RESILIENT

Living, Dying, and Rising
in Rural America

Raymond A. Nadolny, Ph.D.

RESILIENT
Living, Dying, and Rising in Rural America

ISBN: 978-1-5470-3089-7
(also available for Kindle)

Book design and layout: Lighthouse24
Cover photo: rangizzz/Shutterstock

CONTENTS

FOREWORD
RESILIENT

WHEN I ARRIVED in North Dakota, Barack Obama had just become the 44th president of the United States. The country was in recession and, Williston, a small, rural town in western North Dakota, 18 miles from the Montana border to the west and 60 miles from the Canadian border to the north, experienced an oil boom equivalent to the California Gold Rush. I was so busy trying to survive life in the oil patch that by the time I left, I didn't even realize how divided our country had become.

For seven years, I served as president of a state college in the midst of an unprecedented economic boom many times the size of a boom only a couple of decades earlier. On my arrival in early 2009, oil was at record lows. Not many in Williston remembered the prior boom and bust of the late 1980s fondly. It was devastating to Williston and the surrounding oil counties. During that boom, legislators used the new-found wealth to fund K-12 education while no such assistance was provided to oil counties struggling to expand services. When the boom went bust, the legislature addressed the school district deficits while the small city of Williston was left with $25M in debt which they were still paying off twenty-five years later.

No one was predicting another boom yet history would soon repeat itself. As the boom of 2009 picked up speed, both my family and the community are taken for the ride of our lives. I witnessed a rural community emerge from decades of depression to become the nation's economic hot spot for just over five years. I saw that same community then descend into a recession in less than a year.

The story of this latest boom and bust is both wonderful and tragic. Neglected, even abused, the players are heroes, fools, and martyrs. My personal story involves my college's relationship with a strip club, state scandals (one of which ends in suicide), a sex offender on campus, and even my temporary exile at the hands of the university system. Each chapter takes another step down the rabbit's hole.

The comic and tragic nature of the 2009 oil boom informs us why a pipeline protest in North Dakota can take place and even why a character like Donald J. Trump was elected president. I don't write specifically about the North Dakota pipeline or the election of President Trump, but in telling my story, I learned the why's of both. Nine out of ten voters in Williston, North Dakota voted for Donald Trump. The divide is real. If the election taught urban America anything, it's that we need to listen to what is taking place in rural America. And in a market dominated by urban consumers, stories from America's heartland seem to be far and in-between. People have grown comfortable reading stories about themselves. But will we pay the price for such self-indulgence?

Williston, existing in a rustic bubble, is an excellent lens through which to view the rural-urban divide. The oil boom in 2009 magnified the contrast between the living conditions of urban versus rural. With the national recession in full force, people from larger cities flocked to the small town hoping to take advantage of the city's newfound wealth. Investment dollars poured in, sending the prices of real estate and local services soaring. Many locals, especially apartment dwellers whose rents doubled overnight, found they could no longer afford their homes. A mass exodus of senior citizens took place, many of whom were born and raised in Williston.

The government did little to protect this community under siege. The university system turned its back. Oil companies arrived in corporate jets carrying high paid Washington, D.C. charity consultants, making a pretense of caring. The philanthropic mark left by one New York headquartered company can now only be found in their pocketbooks. And what started so suddenly would end just as quickly. When America's economy began to rebound again, Williston's economy hit the floor. My presidency went from joy to heartbreak to surrender to endurance to hope.

But the resilience of a community neglected for generations, its skepticism of government, and its "do-it-on-your-own" mentality taught me about the greatness and the baseness of a segment of the population that would ultimately change the expected outcome of our presidential election. The experience taught me how little we know about each other, how little we understand about each other, and how much there is to appreciate about each other.

Chapter 1
NORTH DAKOTA

"We're not in a recession, we're in a slowdown."

—President George W. Bush, April 22, 2008

SURVIVAL OF THE FITTEST

Few know the real story behind Williston, North Dakota. They couldn't. The press turned Williston into a sort of Pulp Fiction. True, those reporters were given plenty of ammunition – a silver platter laden with the bizarre and the unnatural.

Journalists creatively wove urban myths into rural myths. Stories included everything from six-figure jobs, oil spills, crime and prostitutes. The tales, better fit for scandal sheets, were made "decent" by "respected" media outlets like the Associated Press, the *New York Times*, and CNN. Social media did not have to do much more than spread them across the country.

Still, the oil rush is a story of biblical proportions, full of prophets, martyrs, tax collectors, plagues, miracles, and strippers. One had to live and survive the Williston experience to appreciate the complexities of the city's boom cycle. But in early 2009, when I became Williston State's third president, there was little press. Most people, including those in the state of North Dakota, took neither interest nor notice in this tiny community almost bankrupted from the first boom.

The Land that Time Forgot

"North Dakota: We Really Are One of the 50 States"

—North Dakota State Slogan

My announcement of a presidency in North Dakota to my friends and coworkers in the Seattle area had the same effect as letting people know I was going on an overseas mission. People stared. Their mouths remained open for an uncomfortable period. No one knew what to say. A simple "Congratulations" would have been nice. The response was more often: "North Dakota?" North Dakota was not deemed civilization.

People would point out that North Dakota was one of the five to six remaining states they had yet to visit. They had no idea about the quixotic realities—like oil, crime, and exotic dancers—that would later establish Williston's reputation. Knowledge of North Dakota could be summarized in the movie *Fargo*: cold, primitive, wide open spaces, and a strange accent that portrayed people like a lost Amish family that settled too far north.

Selling the Idea

While I know the standard claim is that Yosemite, Niagara Falls, the upper Yellowstone and the like, afford the greatest natural shows, I am not so sure but the Prairies and Plains, while less stunning at first sight, last longer, fill the esthetic sense fuller, precede all the rest, and make North America's characteristic landscape.[1]

—Walt Whitman

I successfully sold my family on leaving the comforts of Seattle for the rural but majestic hardships of the Northern Great Plains. It was to be a three-year commitment. My wife Joyce's Ivy League background and success in the IT industry left her open to a new adventure.

My young daughters were equally up for the adventure. Kiana and Sophia, my step-children, were in third and fifth grade. Julia was two years old, and Emma was just over a month. I did my research. The case for Williston, North Dakota was strong.

Williston was the boyhood home of Phil Jackson. He led Williston High School's basketball team to two state titles. The NBA Hall of Famer, Chicago Bulls coach and Los Angeles Lakers coach revisited his alma mater to the delight of the nearly 13,000 residents – all of whom seemed to possess a Phil Jackson story.

North Dakota was ranked the most outgoing state, one of the top ten most livable states and was one of the top ten states for child well-being. Williston ranked 53rd in *Midwest Living Magazine's* 2008 "Top 100 Small Town Getaways." *The Outdoorsmen* consistently ranked Williston highly in its top 200 Towns: 24th in 2009.

North Dakota was even a leader in education: second highest high school graduation rate in the nation; the third highest rate of students who pursue higher education; ranked fourth by *Education Week* in overall K-12 achievement. And unlike the years that would follow, North Dakota was the third safest state in the nation.

The story of North Dakota is a historian's dream. The state was first settled several thousand years ago by Native Americans. The Missouri-Yellowstone Confluence Center and historic Fort Buford is a stone's throw from the majestic and beautiful Theodore Roosevelt National Park, commonly referred to as the Badlands.

In the late 19th century, Fort Buford protected trading interests and immigrants settling in the West. It is probably best remembered for the famous Hunkpapa Sioux leader, Sitting Bull, who returned to surrender his rifle in 1881. Four years earlier, Chief Joseph and the Nez Perce were housed at Fort Buford as prisoners after their defeat at the Battle of the Bear Paw Mountains in Montana.

The Fort Union Trading Post, another legacy of the Old West also sits in Williston's backyard. It lays claim to being the most famous fur trading post on the Upper Missouri River, having witnessed the inauguration of steamboat transportation on the Big Muddy.

Williston even has a romantic side. During the Lewis and Clark expedition in 1805, Meriwether Lewis identified the area as "...this long wished for spot."

American Made

I was born in a very small town in North Dakota, a town of only about 350 people. I lived there until I was 13. It was a marvelous advantage to grow up in a small town where you knew everybody.

Warren Christopher[2]

The response from my wife was incredible. Joyce, a 5'1" Asian American, incredibly beautiful, and with the energy level of a supernova, wanted to move to North Dakota. I was stunned.

Joyce grew up in a bedroom community outside of New York City. She spoke with a thick New Jersey accent—although she modified it to what sounded like a California Valley Girl during her undergraduate years at Harvard. Joyce was both practical and adaptable.

Her imagination ran wild when thinking about the Great Plains. Wholesome food and homemade everything – an entire community made up of Martha Stewarts before she was "Martha Stewart." The people would be creative, resourceful, hard working, and ethical.

Joyce believed she would be among "her people." In college (Harvard), she was the lone knitter. She would frequent the yarn store in Cambridge, never seeing a classmate even though the shop was in the heart of campus. Joyce had no peers to share her passion. In North Dakota, she hoped to add quilting to her repertoire of traditional crafts.

She heard that in the Midwest, people looked out for each other, took care of each other. She heard stories of kindness and generosity, frugality and resourcefulness. Joyce was looking for an adventure.

North Dakota fit the bill perfectly. With a newborn and three small girls in hand, she too would be a pioneer, living off the land and making lifelong friends.

I wanted to be president. Joyce believed she would encounter kindred spirits. Our excuses knew no bounds.

The sun had been hiding in Seattle for the past ten years. With 202 sunny days a year in North Dakota, even the legendary cold could not dampen my enthusiasm. It would feel good to feel the sun again in its full North Dakota glory.

The Final Interview

"I have always said I would not have been President had it not been for my experience in North Dakota."

Theodore Roosevelt

Stepping off the airplane, I looked out at an endless frozen landscape. Each breath immediately froze in the negative 45 degree temperature. I felt energized.

The North Dakota State Board of Higher Education had scheduled their normal monthly meeting in Williston to conduct the final interview for the Williston State College president. Many State Board members and many of the state's presidents did not attend. For those that did attend, most phoned into the meeting.

I did not believe the State Board would hire another male president. The Chancellor was male. Ten of the eleven presidents in the university system were male with the eleventh president yet to be hired. But I did not yet understand North Dakota, a rural state with values rooted in the 1950s. Diversity considerations were hardly a factor in the State Board's decision-making.

I was a finalist at two other colleges, too, so my prospects of finding a presidency felt good. I stepped into the interview with a strong air of confidence. I cannot say if I performed better than the other candidates, but I was confident of my chances of landing a role (if not at Williston State, then in one of the other colleges in which I was a finalist).

The previous president, after eight years in the role, received a vote of no confidence by the faculty. I did not hear a lot of interest or enthusiasm about the college from the State Board, the people responsible for the hiring. The atmosphere was decidedly low-key. Then the snow started falling.

During the interviews, a fierce blizzard moved into the area, and the airport closed. The city shut down. As such, there was little motivation to drag out the hiring much longer. The newly selected president would stay, negotiate a contract, and get to know the community. The candidates not selected would return to their hotels and wait for a flight out of town.

I was selected as Williston State's third president and immediately accepted the job. With oil hovering at $35.00 a barrel, no one could have warned me of the door I had opened. The North Dakota in which I arrived, the city of Williston in which my family and I would now live, the college I would grow to love, was neither the city nor the school I would leave.

Booms do that. Booms force change. Booms make you grow whether you want to or not.

I love North Dakota. But like all love affairs, there is both love and hate. North Dakota can be a real bitch.

—

THE NORTHERN GREAT PLAINS

"My grandmother raised five children during the Depression by herself. At 50, she threw her sewing machine into the back of a pickup truck and drove from North Dakota to California. She was a real survivor, so that's my stock. That's how I want my kids to be too."

Michelle Pfeiffer[3]

A Rough Start

Even before arriving, I inadvertently panicked the college. With a little over one hundred employees, I requested the employee job descriptions be emailed to me. What I did not realize, could not even fathom, was that most of the employees did not have written job descriptions.

Panic swept through the campus as employees attempted to scratch out job descriptions to meet the "demand" of the incoming president. Two weeks after the request, still blissfully ignorant of the situation, I sent a follow-up email again requesting the job descriptions. What was the holdup?

Almost immediately, I received half of the job descriptions; some were handwritten. I was promised the rest the following week. I had unintentionally opened a can of worms.

Not even on the job, I had made my first mistake: I made an assumption. The assumption was incorrect, and people panicked, fearing for their jobs and their future. There was much I did not know. I would have to find a way to accelerate through what would quickly become a steep learning curve.

Fortunately, one of the reasons I took the position was the size of the college. As a new president, if problems arose, I could easily walk to an office and have a one-on-one conversation. Lessons could be learned, mistakes could be remedied, and misunderstandings resolved through communication. I was still excited.

I had spent eight years in seminary training to be a priest. I served as a chaplain in a hospital. I had taken teens to Mexico and Appalachia to build houses. I had never lost my love of service. I told my wife it felt no different from going on a mission. I thought I was more than prepared having spent the last twenty-five years in higher education leadership. I felt ready, and in the changing and chaotic world of Williston, it seemed I could not have chosen a better place to make a difference.

Norwegian Ancestry

"Either conform to the customs or flee the country."

Norwegian Proverb[4]

I learned very quickly that even though I had grown up in the Midwest, the culture of the Northern Great Plains is both unique and foreign. In North Dakota, one in three residents is of Norwegian heritage."[5] Thirty-seven percent of people living in Williston are of Norwegian descent.[6]

Norwegians immigrated to the United States in the latter half of the 19th century. The Great Plains was to the farmer what the Bakken has become to oil companies. From lutefisk (lye-soaked cod) to the Sons of Norway (where I soon became a member), North Dakota boasts a long and proud Norwegian heritage.

North Dakota, and especially western North Dakota, with brief booms in the 1950s and 1980s, had been struggling since the Great Depression. The people of the Northern Great Plains learned a long time ago to cast a blind eye to neglect. It is how they survive.

North Dakotans in the post-depression era endured withering storms, fierce winds, substandard infrastructure, little to no health care services, and declining educational systems. Williston, geographically isolated, was worse off than most. The college was no different.

Terry Olson

The first two people I met were Terry Olson and Lance Olson, not related. Terry Olson, the director of the Williston State College Foundation, looked like a garden gnome without the beard, while Lance Olson, a science professor, looked like the Marlboro Man without the cigarette. Both possessed North Dakota's trademark self-effacing humor.

Terry was everyone's favorite but extremely mischievous uncle and the reason I came to North Dakota. He was responsible for the college's athletic facility built five years earlier. The facility boasted the highest sports attendance for any community college in the country. *The Well*, as it was called, was the only game in town. If a community could build such a complex almost entirely on its own dime, there was more here than met the eye.

Nothing brought me more pleasure than watching Terry engage people. He was a virtual comedic punching bag. Everybody, from small children to the elderly delighted in taunting him. Whether you were being assaulted by Terry or the one doing the assaulting, playing with Terry was like playing with a mischievous Norwegian elf.

Terry knew and loved everyone. He could strike up a conversation anywhere and with anybody. Terry was related to everyone by one to two degrees of separation. He would finish by recounting numerous personal stories, quickly installing himself as more than an acquaintance. Terry was downright incestuous.

Terry was also the heart of Williston, the walking, breathing personification of the community. Any major decision I made I ran through Terry, and he regularly steered me away from potential land mines. He became a trusted advisor and friend.

As my family would not be joining me until after the two older girls completed the school year in Washington, Terry invited me to share Easter dinner at his home. Looking up his address in the phone book, I scrolled through pages of Olsons. Olson appeared to be the Norwegian equivalent of "Smith."

At dinner, Terry immediately launched into a litany of Lena and Ole jokes. For the uninitiated, Lena and Ole are politically incorrect characters in a line of Scandinavian jokes[7]:

> Ole only has a few hours left to live. Lying in bed, he smells something. Cake. Chocolate cake, his favorite! He crawls out of bed and drags himself to the kitchen.
>
> When Lena walks in, there is Ole, sitting at the kitchen table, eating cake. She hollers at him, "Ole!

What are you doing in here? You're sick! You should be in bed! You shouldn't be out here eating cake! That's for the funeral!"

Terry had already accomplished what would have been a proud legacy for any living soul. But it was nothing compared to what he would do over the next seven years. When so many city elders would leave Williston, Terry remained. When the community was in turmoil, Terry didn't flinch. Terry embraced a community set on fire.

Lance Olson: Rite of Passage

"I do not believe there ever was any life more attractive to a vigorous young fellow than life on a cattle ranch in those days. It was a fine, healthy life, too; it taught a man self-reliance, hardihood, and the value of instant decision...I enjoyed the life to the full."

Teddy Roosevelt

On meeting Lance Olson, my optimism ascended to an all-time high. Lance has deep roots in the community. Lance's father was superintendent of schools. His dad played a significant role in the life of Phil Jackson. His family owns property directly across from the Theodore Roosevelt National Park, 60 miles south of Williston.

Lance trained as a geologist and held mineral rights. "Mineral rights," as newcomers to Williston quickly learned, allow the owner to receive royalties from the oil beneath the land. During the boom, Lance could have easily walked away from teaching, but like Terry, his passion kept him at the college. Lance built his home, an incredible log cabin, sitting atop of the basin overlooking the city. He wasn't going anywhere.

Lance is also a cowboy, the real deal. He trained his horse to ride up and down the steep grades of the Badlands in the same manner as the Native Americans. Lance is a man's man.

Giving me the opportunity to return to the land and "earn my spurs," Lance invited me to brand cattle. Growing up in the Chicago suburbs, I could never have imagined myself branding cattle.

The gruesome process involved bringing a calf to the ground, cutting off its testes, and burning the helpless creature with a hot iron. As a newbie, I would not have to do the more repugnant work. It was left to the professionals to cut off the testes and work the hot iron.

The college's baseball team joined Lance and me at the ranch. Recruited from places like New York and California, they were given the job of finding a calf, bringing it to the ground and then holding the animal down so the "real cowboys" could do their work. The sight of the baseball players chasing the calves was like a "Three Stooges" movie. The baseball players, tall and lanky, found themselves falling over each other in their efforts to catch a calf. Easier said than done.

After watching Lance clip the testes, I momentarily doubted my commitment to eating meat. I would never eat another steak or hamburger ever, I swore to myself. That moment, thankfully, was brief. I dropped the first calf I saw. The calf was clipped and branded.

Blood was on the ground, and the smell of burnt flesh was in the air. It was like a cowboy rite of passage.

I shared my branding experience with my vegetarian family. On a positive note, my heavily edited version helped to reaffirm my family's commitment to a vegetarian lifestyle. On a more unfortunate note, northwest North Dakota would be a difficult place for them to maintain their meat-free lifestyle.

Lance rewarded my initiation into cattle branding with a visit to several teepee rings on his property. The Lakota Indians, a migratory people, used the site for their summer buffalo hunts. Ten to twenty feet in diameter and hundreds of years old, each of the 20 odd rings were a single line of boulders. The cluster of stone circles was magnificent and, according to Lance, could be seen from space.

During the day, one could see for miles in any direction. The vistas reach from the great Missouri River to the Canadian skyline. Or as my wife heard from a college employee: "Welcome to North Dakota, where you can watch your dog running away for three days."

At night, one had the most magnificent views of the heavens. Lance was not a religious man, but he was sharing with me a uniquely spiritual experience. I was feeling a part of the great American West. The outdoors, the culture, the history was capturing my imagination and heart. I had abandoned the status and trappings of Nordstrom for the practicality of Walmart. I was starting to buy into a simpler lifestyle. Yes, it was rough. But what greater opportunity existed, I thought, than serving a college in the Northern Great Plains?

—

VOLUNTEER

"In 1862, President Abraham Lincoln signed the Homestead Act and created opportunity for the 372,000 families that poured onto the prairies. The families came for many reasons – a hunger for land, a vision for the future, a longing for adventure, or an interest in profit. Some failed. Some scraped by. Some succeeded and, in the process, put down roots that shaped the region as we know it."[8]

Ndstudies.org

Instant Civilization

The Great Plains' vast and unfriendly landscape was daunting to the first settlers. So how does one make the inhospitable hospitable? Professor Richard Stenberg, the college's history professor, provided me with the answer. Pioneers, eager to make a home, created what was called "instant civilization." Instant civilization sprang up everywhere pioneers settled. And nowhere are the examples more prevalent than in the cities scattered across North Dakota.

Harsh winters and fierce winds, an open landscape that jutted out in any direction as far as the eye could see, settlers were in the business of "talking up" their towns. The small towns needed talking up. Life was hard. Resources were limited. The population seemed to be in perpetual decline.

The small towns presented the image of being a city in the hopes of one day attracting enough people to turn the image into reality. Churches, schools, and town halls could be found in even the smallest towns. Most towns could not support a store in the conventional sense. But one would find a "store" stocked with necessary supplies. Most had no staff, but a notebook sat next to the till in which people would write what goods they were purchasing. An astonishing number of towns even had mini opera houses. Even the state's Capitol building is an example of instant civilization. The impressive twenty-one story building was built in 1931. Ten of the twenty-one stories remained vacant for years.

Traces of instant civilization can still be seen throughout western North Dakota. It was the last part of the state to settle, the last part of the state to have roads. Even today, Western North Dakota remains a western territory more in common with the early 20th century than the 21st century.

Volunteer City

The cities, scant on every imaginable resource, survived on volunteerism. Williston possessed all the qualities of a volunteer city: volunteer mayor, volunteer fire department, and service organizations galore. Ward Koeser was Williston's volunteer mayor for 20 years.

Ward would oversee the fastest growing micropolitan in the country. While other cities experienced only a sliver of the explosive oil patch growth, Williston faced the coming storm with a cadre of dedicated volunteers. Ward knew full well the boom-bust cycle.

Ward became mayor in 1994 when the city was dealing with the fallout left from the last bust. With a declining population and an infrastructure in shambles, he led through bad times and good times. And for most of his term, he led on his own dime. Ward owned his own business. So when the boom was in full force, Ward handed over the day-to-day operations of his business to one of his employees and became a full-time volunteer mayor.

Howard Klug, Williston's current volunteer mayor, is another example of volunteerism. When Klug was a city commissioner and running for the city's mayor, United States Senator Heidi Heitkamp set up a dinner for Howard to meet a visiting senator from Delaware. Howard Klug, the city commissioner, would be meeting with two United States senators. Like most politicians, the senators arrived late. Over dinner, the three discussed the boom and its impact on the country. But at quarter to nine, Howard excused himself. He had volunteered to be the doorman at the Moose Lodge starting at 9 pm. So at 8:45 pm, Howard called the dinner with the U.S. senators short to make his volunteer commitment.

Both Ward and Howard worked as part-time mayors when billions of dollars in oil revenues came into Williston. The mayor and the city council dealt with roads, sewer, housing, and healthcare. They were also busy volunteering in service clubs, their respective churches, and even the fire department. When Councilman Brad Bekkedahl, a full-time dentist and a full colonel in the National Guard became a state senator, he chose to remain in his volunteer position on the city council. He hired another dentist to lighten his workload.

Being a good neighbor is at the heart of volunteerism. People trust one another and look out for each other. I saw this principle in action during my first trip to Walmart. When I parked my car, I was amazed at the number of cars unlocked and left running in the parking lot. There was no thought of theft as row upon row of empty cars spewed exhaust.

Coming from Seattle and Chicago, the cars would have been stolen in a heartbeat.[9] In North Dakota, neighborly is a way of life. Neighbors share; neighbors give help when you need it. From the city's "Band Day" to Fourth of July celebrations, people focus on the interests of the community.

Being a good neighbor was not just words. On more than one occasion, while we were out of town, people came to our house and ploughed our large driveway and sidewalks. We were all in it together. People would get a church started. People would build a school. There was no waiting for the state. There was no waiting for federal dollars. The city was highly parochial but also highly loyal. No one was going to advance these isolated communities except for the community itself.

This remarkable sense of self-reliance would be critical given future events. Over six years, Williston would transition from 13,000 people to over 35,000 people. The city would experience the sharpest labor and housing shortage in the country. Even with these changes, the fire department, the mayor, the state's legislature would remain as they were – volunteers. It would only be after the boom that the city council would finally approve their first full-time paid city manager.

Volunteer Legislature

North Dakota may have the largest government per capita, but the government is filled with volunteers. Park districts, library districts, the State Board of Higher Education are all volunteers. North Dakota is a volunteer state.

North Dakota legislators are not career politicians. Being a legislator is not how they make their living. In North Dakota, the general feeling is that legislators experience what citizens experience. Representative Skarphol worked for an oil company.

Representative Carlson was a contractor. The clear majority of North Dakota legislators are ranchers, farmers, small business owners, architects, educators, and insurance agents.

Having spent most my career in Illinois, Oregon, Arizona and Washington, I had no idea of volunteer legislators. Legislators in my previous experiences had offices. In North Dakota, legislators shared a common desk in the assembly hall. While it was difficult to spend any meaningful time with legislators in states like Illinois and Washington, I would become fast friends with legislators in North Dakota.

If I had understood the concept of a volunteer legislature earlier, I would have saved myself a lot of the stress over legislator's public information requests. Because legislators did not have a staff to do research, they filed public information requests. The time to respond to public information requests was an enormous task, especially for a small college with limited resources. The university system took the requests and the resulting workload personally. But for the most part, I came to understand, the public information requests were just an effective way for legislators with no staff to get information.

Legislative Power

In North Dakota's legislature, power was easy to identify. The center of power in North Dakota tended to be in the center of the state (Bismarck) and in the eastern part of the state (Grand Forks and Fargo). However, northwest North Dakota, to my surprise, had power, at least in the state legislature. The power's name was Representative Bob Skarphol. Representative Skarphol was a farmer and oil contractor. He served on the House's most powerful committee, appropriations. As chair of the House's Higher Education Committee, he was a major force both in the legislature and the university system.

Within my first month, Representative Skarphol hijacked my office. Unbeknownst to me, he had called a meeting. I only found out about the meeting after I arrived at my office. Smiling and gently rocking back and forth in my chair, Representative Skarphol smiled and let me know he had been waiting for me.

Representative Gary Sukut, Representative Pat Hatlestad, and Senator Stan Leeson were sitting next to him. I had obviously arrived late. As the group hovered around Skarphol, I immediately knew who was in charge and took one of the seats I usually made available to guests.

The power structure in North Dakota is not complicated. Power in the Legislature centers around three people: the governor, the House member in charge of management, and the Senate member in charge of management. Although Skarphol was not in charge of management, there are typically five to six people that make an inner circle around the management leader. In the state's House of Representatives, Skarphol was a member of that inner circle.

As a member of the management circle, he ensured a piece of the budget pie would always come home to western North Dakota. One month after I arrived in Williston, the session ended, and Skarphol was present to announce the college's share: 1. Permission for bonding to build a $10.5 million residence hall, 2. $1.7 million for science building renovation, and 3. $5.3 million dollars to build a Career and Technical Training Center. The State Board did not have to make a request to the legislature for the projects. The college did not have to lobby for them. Skarphol's legislative clout just pushed them through.

The meeting in my office was just to make sure I did not "screw up" the projects. Skarphol, an independent oil contract pumper and a farmer, had just been named Legislator of the Year by the North Dakota Association of Oil and Gas Producing Counties. Skarphol was well informed on higher education and probably attended more national education conferences then the average college president. He was an outspoken critic of North Dakota's higher education system, and unpopular with the various college presidents as he did not hesitate to make open records requests to the University System.

The most influential person in the oil patch, Skarphol possessed a level of clout never before held in northwest North Dakota. Skarphol's meeting in my office was quite simply a courtesy call to the new guy. Skarphol wanted to make sure his projects were completed in such a way as to afford him bragging rights during the next session.

At the time, I did not understand Skarphol's position in the legislature. As a new president, there was no orientation, much less a primer on how it all worked. The chancellor simply stayed out of the way, and I was pretty much expected to do the same.

Just two months into my job, Representative Al Carlson, the House member in charge of management and the real power in the House of Representatives would rake me over the coals at a joint budget section meeting. I did not know it at the time, but it was the habit of the legislature to place sitting presidents on the hot seat, regardless of the issue. I thought I had come with an important issue, but once again I tripped up culturally as I ran into another case of North Dakota volunteerism.

In keeping with North Dakota's volunteer fashion and out of necessity, I assigned a project manager for each of Skarphol's capital projects. The college had no deans, no assistants, no human resource director. There was no identified head of the custodians. Each person the college selected as a project manager would be volunteering. The athletic director would serve as the project manager for the $10.5 million residence hall. A sociology instructor would act as the project manager for the $5.3 million Career and Technology Center. And Lance Olsen would serve as the project manager for the $1.7 million science renovation.

The volunteers had neither the background nor the experience for the job. There was no pay. The university system had neither an architect nor a construction manager to assist them. It was North Dakota business as usual.

As an outsider, I found the situation absurd. My mistake was in thinking that I could change directions and hire a professional to run the $17.5 million in combined projects. I went to the legislative budget section to request permission to hire one full-time person to manage the three projects. I was laughed out of the room.

Representative Carlson accused me of wanting to add another full-time employee to the college that would never go away. Request denied. Ill-equipped faculty and staff volunteers would remain responsible for the construction of $17.5 million in capital projects.

The Curmudgeons

For the House leadership, in which I include Representative Skarphol, I created my own nickname: the Curmudgeons. Cantankerous, crusty, and conservative, House leadership acted closer to the machinations of the French revolution. They trusted no one. There was a sort of mob mentality.

Carlson, like Robespierre, handed out assignments. A chosen few ran the most important committees like Appropriations. Anyone that stood in their way would be shown the guillotine. Higher education, I would learn, was always on the chopping block.

With no professional staff to support them, social media played an increasingly dominant role in how legislators received information. When legislators were not in committee, they were sitting at their desks in the assembly hall. Each one had some type of desktop, tablet, or smartphone and could be seen surfing the internet, checking Facebook or trolling for the most recent news reports on their activities. President Trump is only the latest incarnation of this group.

The general feeling was that North Dakota government did not need to be big. The state had weathered decades of population decline. That was okay. With less money in the coffers, volunteers picked up extra jobs.

Requests from state agencies for money to hire more people went contrary to the volunteer nature of the state. The requests were not only rejected but also met with legislative disdain. In highly rural and historically poor states like North Dakota, big government did not work. Big government was not trusted.

Chancellor Goetz understood the tension that existed between the legislature and the university system. The university system and legislature were frenemies. The system was broken, and the safest bet was to avoid conflict. And for Chancellor Goetz, his biggest asset was Laura Glatt, his vice chancellor of finance.

Most presentations to the legislature were made by Laura Glatt, who also bore the brunt of the legislative beatings. A public servant who served for decades, Laura kept a dysfunctional university system running through unwavering perseverance. Laura was both champion and martyr of the university system.

On my first meeting with the chancellor, he made it clear to me what was important: positive press. Each time we met, he asked how many good news stories made it into the papers. If the goal was to fly under the radar, the chancellor was the master. The two unspoken rules were that you never confronted the legislature head on and, if at all possible, you did not make your own fiscal requests. The chancellor behaved like a benevolent father. Kind but strict, you knew you did not want to make dad mad.

The two later chancellors hired from outside of the state would learn quickly about the dysfunctional relationship between the university system and the legislature. Each made legislative requests for additional staff. The legislature's response: reductions to the university system's staff.

North Dakota is a volunteer state. North Dakota is one big family. The four-hundred-mile main street means everyone is a neighbor. Church is not separate from state. Work is not separate from home. Personal is not separate from professional. Everyone lends a hand. Unfortunately, there just aren't enough hands.

Chapter 2
MAKING A DIFFERENCE

"When my parents first arrived there, North Dakota had just been admitted to the Union, and the country was still wild and harsh."

— Lawrence Welk[10]

PRE-BOOM

The boom would not begin until six months after I arrived. So I had a little time to get to know the state before all the madness set in. Professor Richard Stenberg put North Dakota in perspective for me. Born and raised in Watford City, 30 miles southeast of Williston, Richard was North Dakota's Blarney Stone. Blessed with the gift of the gab, Richard's uncanny knowledge of world and especially North Dakota history earned him the nickname of "Rainman."

I first met Richard at a college symposium on the buffalo. Attendees had the opportunity to taste buffalo tongue and listen to a variety of perspectives on the rise and fall of the buffalo in North Dakota. A master teacher, Richard has that rare gift of making history come alive. A Renaissance man, Richard also introduced me to Aquavit, a distilled Norwegian liquor, pale in color and tasting of anise.

Richard worked as a park ranger at Fort Union during the summer. He had me volunteer at Fort Union driving carts during Rendezvous Days, a reenactment of the 19th century Missouri fur trade. Over time, I graduated from driver to reenactor. Like Lance and Terry, this incredible man of Norwegian ancestry welcomed me into the community, debuted me as a volunteer, and baptized me as a North Dakotan.

But I was still seen as an outsider. Oil was sitting at $35 a barrel, and Williston was struggling to pay off the debt from the last boom. I was just another person coming in to "fix" something that wasn't broken. People sarcastically asked when the new president was leaving.

I purchased the most expensive house in town. The community and my family needed to know that I was committed. Leaving the comforts of the city, I also wanted to make sure my family had as easy an adjustment as possible.

The three-story, brick home was perfect for entertaining. The house was within eyeshot of the campus. I reasoned that if I improved the college, I would improve the value of my home. I could have relaxed and done nothing. The oil boom would soon do it for me.

My neighbor across the street, an oil worker, lost his job the same time I was moving into the neighborhood. A month later, he would drive home in a new F-110 pick-up truck as a signing bonus for his new job. The boom, although we didn't know it at the time, had begun. It was a commonly held belief that this boom, like the last one, would be short lived. They could not have been more wrong.

To complicate matters, Joyce was delayed in leaving Seattle. She called me badly shaken. Joyce's ex-husband sued to have the two older girls remain in Washington. North Dakota might be a leader in education but Williston, we learned from the lawsuit, was not. Joyce was terrified the children would not be able to come out to North Dakota. We had never lived apart and Emma, the youngest, was only four months old.

Baby, toddler, and two small girls in tow, Joyce took control. The owner of the Purple School, a leader in early childhood language education, Joyce's passion was education, and she would use it to her advantage. The suit was settled in Joyce's favor, but the hearings took place over several months. The family would not join me until the end of summer. The lawsuit was the first of several events that would open our eyes to some new realities.

Take the bugs, for instance. No one from Williston bothered to mention that I had relocated to the "Mosquito Capital of the World"... that is, until after my arrival. The sheer number of these insects was staggering, not to mention their persistence. The insects of mythic numbers and proportions were mentioned by Meriwether Lewis, who had issued a warning several hundred years earlier: "The mosquitoes are exceedingly troublesome."

Then there was the weather. A dry climate, the wind in North Dakota can turn temperatures from negative five degrees to negative 45 degrees in a matter of moments. Only later did I realize there was no wind when I interviewed. North Dakota wind is notorious. It can rip the skin off your back. If I wasn't worried about a large mosquito carrying off my child, I was worried about swirling dust making it difficult for her to breathe.

Williston was a veritable dust bowl. Farmers had removed grass to plant their crops, and the resulting dust swept across the Great Plains. Buried under four feet of snow during the interviews, I could not have imagined the neglect, isolation, and dust experienced by the college. As the snow melted, a college, partially in ruins, emerged. Like most things in northwest North Dakota, the campus had never been renovated. Mechanical systems were always in danger of breaking down. And dust sifted into everything.

Dust would roll in like the fog, partially blocking the sun. During my first summer, I spent days washing it off the interior walls. One night, when I left a window cracked open in my office, I returned the next day to find my desk covered in dust. As I traced my finger through the quarter-inch thick layer, I couldn't help but feel that something ominous was taking place in northwest North Dakota. Romanticism was slowly being replaced by reality. I had never lived in a rural community so far from a city. I had failed to read the obvious handwriting on the wall. Until the boom, no one had paid any attention to this tiny community.

Geographically Isolated

Williston State is the only higher education opportunity in northwest North Dakota as well as parts of eastern Montana. The closest Universities are Minot State University; 126 miles (2 hours and 25-minute drive) and Dickinson State University: 131 miles (2 hours and 29-minute drive). North Dakota roads are notoriously long. And with miles upon miles of grassland and farms, long distance travel is a way of life.

When my daughters were old enough to play sports, the away games were anywhere from 45 minutes away to seven hours away. The distance to the average away game was a three-hour one-way trip. The girls took a bus to the game, played, and returned the same day. I was amazed at the number of parents traveling several hours each direction with their children to attend the games.

Many of the games the college played were in Montana and Minnesota. The college's travel budget was unbelievable. But sports were such an important part of these small, geographically distant communities that even in this most frugal of communities, no one blinked an eye at the cost.

While sports-related spending got an open purse, basic services were largely unavailable. Just before my arriving, the college's adjunct mental health professor committed suicide. Several months earlier a student committed suicide. No counselor, no grief sessions, the college just carried on. The college was far removed from most major services. Given the lack of professionals in the area, family had to rely on family.

The State Board

The job of taking care of the college belongs to the North Dakota's State Board of Higher Education. The State Board is located hours away from the college. The Board members represent eleven colleges. But not one of the board members, when I arrived, was from northwest North Dakota, and in my seven years there, they came to the college rarely. The State Board was in a position neither to care nor to advance the needs of our college.

My experience with boards in Arizona and Washington differed markedly from North Dakota's State Board. Arizona and Washington boards, the norm for community college boards, are a stunning contrast compared to the documented dysfunctions of North Dakota's university system. Washington has 34 community and technical colleges. Each has its own board, and the board members are appointed by the governor. In Arizona, every community college has its own board, and board members are elected by district voters. In both Arizona and Washington boards, members are hands on and fully invested in their respective colleges.

In North Dakota's case, one board represents not one but eleven colleges. The workload of the State Board is monstrous. The job is impossible.

The University of North Dakota (UND), a level one research university, has both a law school and a school of medicine. UND employs almost 3,000 employees and has an annual budget of $150 million.

North Dakota State University (NDSU), the state's other level one research university, operates the state's agricultural research centers with locations across the state. NDSU employs approximately 2500 employees and has an annual budget of $75 million.

Each of these universities has the size and depth to warrant its own board. How one board can manage both universities in addition to four regional universities and five community colleges is unfathomable. The lack of board member attendance for my final interview should have been an early warning sign. Several board members had not and would never step foot on the Williston State Campus. The closest board member was from Minot, a two-hour drive from the college. The very people meant to protect the college would indeed neglect it.

Before my arrival, following the vote of no confidence in Williston State's previous president, the college was exposed to all sorts of risks. I stepped into a college where money was and would be a huge problem. The college had negative cash balances in multiple accounts, it was consistently late in making payments, and it consistently misreported finance information. The college's facilities, the vast majority over forty years old with never a renovation, suffered severe neglect with no backup systems. And students increasingly did not want to attend the college. Declining college enrollments over multiple years had put the school's very viability in question. So it was not surprising when the consultant recommended to me that I terminate all of the administrators.

What role did the State Board play in turning around this small college? Now that a president had been selected for the small northwest college, the State Board no longer paid attention. It was occupied with other matters.

The Fighting Sioux

"On May 14, 2009, the North Dakota State Board of Higher Education approved a motion directing UND to retire "Fighting Sioux" nickname and logo, effective October 1, 2009."

—Wikipedia[11]

I attended my first board meeting in May of 2009. Race relations with Native Americans were intense. Any assumptions I held about quiet North Dakota were quickly extinguished by the numerous press affiliates attending the Board meeting. I was seated at the front with the other ten university presidents. But for all intents and purposes, both the college and I were invisible.

A controversy had been brewing since 2005 when the National Collegiate Athletic Association (NCAA) identified the "Fighting Sioux" nickname and logo as both "hostile and abusive" of Native Americans. North Dakotans were up in arms. Most felt the NCAA was targeting North Dakotans. Why come after North Dakota when the Fighting Illini, Florida Seminoles, and the Notre Dame Fighting Irish embraced similar stereotypes?

The Board heard testimony for and against the Fighting Sioux nickname. Outsiders and non-Lakota were appalled by the political correctness of the Board's decision. Even the United States Government and the Bureau of Indian Affairs still used the term, referring to the Lakota collectively as the Great Sioux Nation. Once again, I consulted Professor Stenberg.

For 250 years, the Lakota people are described in Great Plains history as a warlike people. If the nickname was the Fighting Lakota, a controversy might have been averted. But Sioux was an Algonquin word, which the Chippewa used to insult the Lakota in the Minnesota River Valley. Even within two of the Lakota reservations, opinion was divided. The Standing Rock Reservation supported the Fighting Sioux nickname; the Spirit Lake Reservation opposed it.

A Native American alum from North Dakota State University testified that at an NDSU home game against UND, NDSU fans turned on him. He was with his son when fans started to curse and taunt him mistaking him as one of UND's Fighting Sioux. The alum was humiliated and shamed in front of both his son and his alma mater.

The controversy was made more tragic by the fact that the State Board had been dealing with the issue since 2005. A decision was finally made four years later at this very board meeting, to retire UND's nickname. The controversy would not die. For another three years, regardless of the state of the college, regardless of the boom, the State Board's attention would always divert to the Fighting Sioux controversy. The state would expend thousands of hours of university system staff, presidents', and state board members' time as well as spend hundreds of thousands of dollars on an issue that probably should have ended prior to my first board meeting.

I also received an education that night on the State Board's priorities. Research universities came first. The three regional universities (Minot, Mayville, and Dickinson) and two community colleges (Bismarck State College and North Dakota State College of Science) were second. The remaining three community colleges, which included Williston State, silently dropped off the table. Occasionally, the board would pick one up from under the table. Two out of three times, it was not good.

Chancellor William Goetz did the impossible job of managing an overextended university system frequently besieged by the legislature. Goetz was a former Dickinson State University business professor and administrator. Goetz served as an assistant Republican floor leader in both the North Dakota House and Senate. He was Chief of Staff to former Republican Governor Ed Schafer and was Hoeven's chief of staff when the board hired him to become chancellor in July of 2007. The chancellor knew the university system, knew that it might well have been beyond repair. But Chancellor Goetz kept it running.

Williston State, tucked away in the farthest corner of the state, removed from all critical services, felt the brunt of the conflict between the university system and the legislature. While the legislature and the university system dueled, the college operated as a third world nation in North Dakota's higher education system. And as with all third world nations, some interesting practices developed.

—

STRIP CLUB PRESIDENT

"At first, the nightly tips were nothing special, but over the past year – thanks to the thousands of men who have flocked here and landed high-paying jobs – she has been making $2,000 to $3,000 a night, about the same amount she would have earned in an entire week in Vegas."

—CNN, October 25, 2010[12]

Doing an online search for "strippers" and "Williston" in the State Capitol was probably not one of my best ideas. But, hey! I was doing research. And as I would learn, there was support for strippers from many sources.

The college's relationship with the strip club scene was known within the university system. The State Board either paid no attention to the college's relationship with the strip club, or the State Board simply did not care enough to express an opinion one way or the other. The college was clearly off the university system's radar.

Press coverage on Williston strippers will attest to the public's fascination with the Williston stripper scene. The nation's preoccupation with a service geared to meet the carnal demands of oil workers was reported like a voyeuristic soap opera. The entertainment would continue when a second strip club opened soon after the boom.

Up until the 1970s, strippers were primarily female and confined to clubs. Today, strippers represent every gender, transgender, personality and temperament one can imagine. Strippers appear in every conceivable venue including one's front door step. Whispers, Williston's first strip club opened at the end of the first boom in the 1980s. Williston strippers and their customers conformed to the stripper scene of the 1970s, being primarily female with male customers. Unlike the 1970s, Williston strippers were no longer confined to clubs. From parties to personal visits, strippers performed anywhere and everywhere. One employer turned a bus into a mobile strip club. He hired strippers for bus trips to support and reward his employees and friends. It seems a good time was hard to come by but easy to create.

The quality of life in the oil boom city was, at first glance, non-existent: "In Williston... workers here overwhelming call this place 'the Wild West'... According to residents and oilfield workers, including Fred, there are only two things to do in Williston: work and drink."[13] The strip clubs held pride of place for the sex- and pleasure- starved oil workers.

During the 1980s boom, Whispers opened on Williston's Main Street. The strip club was kitty corner from the train station and just across the street from the city's chamber of commerce. The presence of the strip club in the heart of a city could almost be mistaken as a welcome sign. Air travel was limited, so most people came via the train, with Whispers being their first experience of the city.

I was intimately familiar with the club, at least from the outside, as the college foundation held the permit to Whispers' gaming concession. North Dakota state laws provide a unique gaming venue for nonprofits. Any organization in North Dakota wanting to conduct a raffle, bingo, sports pool, paddlewheels, twenty-one, or poker required a local charity permit. In Whispers' case, the charity permit came from the Williston State College Foundation.

Holding the permit also meant managing the gaming concessions. Terry Olson, executive director of the Williston State College Foundation, was responsible for managing the foundation's gaming and that included Whispers. Chancellor Goetz told me to keep an eye on Terry. Interestingly, Goetz never mentioned Whispers.

Sure, I was blown away that the clear majority of foundation revenue came through gaming. Yes, I was doubly blown away that one of the gaming establishments was in a strip club. But I was new and had already made my fair share of mistakes. I was not going to rush to judgment or assume a moral expectation. Terry's accomplishments, the respect he held in the community made me realize that any success I would have would come via Terry's deep North Dakotan roots.

Terry was, as I stated previously, the heart and the soul of the community. On the other hand, he could be dangerously politically incorrect. Terry was a master of ethnic humor, from a litany of Ole and Lena jokes to anything that showed its face on late night TV. But what was politically incorrect in Seattle was different than what was politically incorrect in North Dakota. In the Northern Great Plains, I decided to go with my gut. My gut told me Terry Olson was a decent man.

During my interviews for the presidency, even during my first visit with Terry, strip clubs never came up. My first foundation board meeting was an eye popper. By 2015, gaming would produce more than $300,000 in annual revenue. As I sat in stunned silence, the foundation director took the time to explain the foundation's involvement in no less than ten establishments ranging from bars to restaurants – and of course, Whispers.

I asked the foundation if they had ever thought of pulling the permit on Whispers. The consensus was this would eventually happen, but no one was in a rush to do so. It was my first two months on the job. The college was in a state of utter neglect. I decided to let sleeping dogs lie. That is until an Associated Press (AP) reporter called while I was traveling from Williston to Bismarck for a State Board meeting.

The AP reporter introduced himself like someone wanting to form a long-term relationship. "You have four daughters, don't you?" Thinking the reporter was welcoming me to the community or trying to establish a common familial bond, I was caught off guard by his next question: "How does it feel to be a father of four daughters and a president that accepts money from a local strip club?"

I pulled over and spent the next hour trying to make the best of what certainly would be an awkward, if not career-defining moment. Despite my efforts, the results were not stellar – but given the amount of time spent on the phone discussing strip clubs, I concluded that the resulting published quotes were the best one could hope for:

> "I'm not going to make a moral judgment on these businesses," said Williston State College president Raymond Nadolny, who says the revenue helps fund scholarships, facilities and a fledgling hockey program. "If we didn't have this kind of fiscal resources, we wouldn't be able to do these projects," he said. Nadolny said he did not know how much revenue the college gets from strip club.[14]

Neither the State Board nor the chancellor's office contacted me. Papers in North Dakota did not pick up the AP article. The article completely vanished with one exception.

Through Google, I am now forever connected to strip clubs. This would be the first of many such links that tiny little search box would identify and retain over the next seven years. My once sterling reputation would be battered and bruised in this new environment of irresponsible, irreversible, and irredeemable electronic media.

At the next foundation board meeting, the foundation executive director brought forward a request from Heartbreakers. The second (and newest) strip club in town sought a gaming concession permit from the foundation. Everyone laughed.

One board member asked about the annual revenue from Whispers to which the assistant replied, $40,000. The room grew silent as board members silently contemplated doubling that figure. After what seemed to be a disturbing period of quiet, board members erupted into laughter. The answer was still no.

I formally requested that the foundation board revoke Whispers' permit. The board agreed to a six-month deadline to terminate the contract. No one in the community noticed. No article was published, no AP story. The city's visitors and convention bureau stepped in and picked up the lucrative gaming concession.

Miss North Dakota

Williston is a city filled with contradictions. I had only been at the college two months when I received a call from the director of the Miss USA North Dakota Beauty Pageant. To my shock, the pageant was held in Williston, the only city in the state with a strip club.

Williston, at that time, looked like a depressed city out of an old black and white movie. So I was incredulous that the pageant would be held in Williston over, let's say, Bismarck, Grand Forks, or Fargo. And as the college president, I was invited. I was not sure if it was in my best interest to go, but Terry told me the organizers were key community members. I showed up late thinking they might not let me inside. I could not have been more wrong.

I was recognized in part because I was one of the few people who wore a suit on a daily basis. The usher, flashlight in hand, brought me to the second row where I was ceremoniously seated behind the judges. The swimsuit competition had just started. I glanced at the young women walking the stage in swimsuits. I looked up; I looked down. I did not know where my eyes belonged. I settled for an in-depth study of the back of a judge's head. What was I doing here?

Later in the program, contestants talked publically about various ideas to create change and impact the world. I was impressed. I made a mental effort to suspend my moral judgment, and at the end of the show, I would go back stage, greet the organizers, and hopefully learn more.

The pageant director was quick to educate me on the Miss North Dakota pageant. The purpose of the pageant was to recognize potential, reward achievement and promote women. She said women receive fewer academic and merit scholarships than their male counterparts. The Miss North Dakota Pageant was bridging the gap for women seeking scholarships.

I had once again made a judgment too quickly. In the dusty oil town of Williston, an organization with a long legacy, was being used to provide women increased access to education. At the College's next graduation ceremony, I asked Roxana Saberi, who authored a book on her captivity in Iran, to be the college's graduation speaker. Roxana, a journalist in New York, consented. In 1998, Roxana Saberi had won the Miss North Dakota Pageant.

Williston, North Dakota was increasingly becoming a larger and more complex mystery: a dusty oilfield town, the Miss North Dakota Pageant, gaming revenue from a strip club. I was no longer in Kansas, as they say.

Strippers would be a constant subject of articles coming out of Williston during the boom. Whispers and Heartbreakers were better funded than the college. They certainly got more attention than the college. America's obsession with strippers is so overwhelming that every chapter in this book will have some reference to this most ancient of arts.

Williston was about to be taken on a magical carpet ride. Damage caused by the last boom gone bust was now set on a collision course with yet another impending oil boom. And in another year, North Dakota would project a budget surplus of $1 billion while forty-one other states would project budget deficits that year and the next. No one, and that includes the college, was ready for the ride we were about to take.

—

SLUMLORD PRESIDENT

What's North Dakota's Secret? As the country has tipped into a deep recession over the past two years, North Dakota, under the leadership of the nation's longest-serving governor, John Hoeven, has bucked every trend. In 2008, North Dakota's economy grew 7.3%, twice as fast as any other state except Wyoming, which grew 4.4%. By this point, many states in the industrial Midwest, and housing-bubble states like Arizona, Nevada and Florida, were already shrinking.

—*Forbes*, June 30, 2009[15]

My desire for a college presidency blinded me to some obvious realities about Williston State College. Workforce training took place in what looked like a storage shed. Student housing was in a "temporary" building. The campus managed a large trailer park.

The on-campus trailer park housed everything from staff and student housing to childcare and adult education. The conditions on campus were obvious warning signs. I was a slumlord president.

Slumlord Daycare

The college (with the team name of the "Tetons") leased one of the 16 trailers in its trailer park to the unrelated "Little Tetons Daycare." Within my first few months, Child Protective Services informed me that Little Tetons Daycare was under investigation.

Unfortunately, the Tetons name in the child care and the fact that it was situated on campus left an indelible connection in the mind of the community. The community wrongly believed Little Tetons Daycare was a college enterprise. The college immediately gave notice to Little Tetons Daycare that its lease would not be renewed. Child Protective Services pulled its license one month later.

Slumlord Adult Education

The Adult Learning Center was housed in the trailer closest to the college's main building, Stevens Hall. The Center provides adults the opportunity to complete their high school graduation requirements. It was an important and necessary program, yet adult education had been relegated to the least desirable location on campus.

The three-bedroom trailer had been converted into a classroom, an office the size of a closet and a bathroom. A space traditionally designed to meet the unique needs of a diverse set of student learners, our adult education trailer was more suited to house the local rodent population than anything having to do with learning. I had seen and would later purchase FEMA trailers in better condition than the trailer inhabited by the Adult Learning Center.

The bathroom was not soundproof, and the walls were so thin that odors escaped immediately. When a student needed to use the bathroom, the director, Laurel, would ask the 10 to 20 students to vacate the trailer temporarily. When the person finished using the facility – and after a brief buffer window of time to clear the air – the students could then go back into the trailer to continue their studies.

The trailer was first brought to my attention due to a rat infestation. Laurel profusely apologized when bringing the rat problem to my attention, as though it did not warrant a complaint. North Dakotans survived terrible winters, fierce winds, and for many decades, abject poverty. Why would a rat infestation be cause for complaint?

For me, the answer was simple: Move adult education out of the trailer and into the main building. My response – "No, we're not putting together a moving plan. Move now. Move by the end of the week" – was both frustrating and bewildering to a staff and a student body used to decades of neglect.

Several years later, I would be the first college president in North Dakota to receive the Department of Education's Lifelong Learning Outstanding Leadership Award. People told me how proud I must be to receive the award. I was not proud.

Sure, there were other things I had done to advance Adult Education. But I should have been fired for doing anything other than removing students from the rodents' den. Adult Education has a long history of being treated like an unwanted child at community colleges. In North Dakota, adult education was the bastard child.

The staff, the community, the State Board had let this injustice go on for years. The neglect, the abysmal conditions that were accepted as normal for a hardy and, what increasingly became apparent, abused people. I should have been removed from my position if I had done anything else versus any accolades delivered after the fact.

Slumlord Student Housing

I did not visit Dickson Hall, the college's residence hall, until the end of May. I had heard stories of the college's student housing, and when I saw Dickson Hall, it crushed my spirit. There was no way I could make up for decades of neglect in one summer, or one year, or even three years.

Dickson Hall was constructed in 1970 as "temporary" housing for students. Temporary meant a maximum of 10 years. Nearly 40 years later, Dickson Hall remained the main residence hall for students. I do not believe that "temporary" exists in the North Dakota dictionary.

The residence hall had significant structural issues. The interior floor sloped downward. I felt more comfortable walking on the floor of the adult education trailer.

I placed a billiard ball on one end the dorm floor and watched it run from one end to the other. As I walked to retrieve the ball, loud groans, pops and squeaks emanated from below me. I felt like I could step through the floor at any moment.

The exterior walls were cracking. Masonry was falling to the ground. The building had no fire sprinkler. Despite the notoriously hot North Dakota summers, the building had no cooling. Heaters installed in 1991 and 1996 were at the end of their useful life.

A student complaint had brought me to the building. Stepping inside confirmed my worst fears immediately. Furniture was old, dirty and falling apart. I suspected that the mattresses had been there since the opening of the building four decades earlier.

To the chagrin of my staff, I immediately began throwing furniture out the door of Dickson Hall onto the front steps out front. I was incensed. The college mission statement, which I thought trite at the time, was "Where the People Make the Difference."

As I tossed out sofas, tables, chairs and the like, I kept asking in sarcastic tones: "Where the people make the difference? Where the people make the difference?" I am sure those watching and listening thought I was crazy.

At that point, I knew the current mission statement of the college was here to stay. The employees at the college would indeed make the difference. Even if I had to *make* them make the difference.

I would start with making a difference in student housing. Williston State had been authorized bonding to build a new residence hall, although it did not have the fiscal capacity to incur such a debt. The vice president of business affairs and the vice chancellor for the university system recommended against moving forward with the new building. But as I hurled busted furniture out of Dickson Hall, the new residence hall took on a greater sense of urgency. I was done being a slumlord president. I was willing to take a risk.

Staff Slumlord

Loneliness, thy other name, thy one true synonym, is prairie.
—William A. Quayle, *The Prairie and the Sea* (1905)

A number of staff lived in the college trailer park. Trailers ranged from functional to the unlivable. Keith, director of student services, invited me to his trailer. He wanted to let me know first-hand that he had accepted another position out of state. We did not go into his trailer. Instead, Keith handed me a beer and we sat out on lawn chairs in the back looking out over the prairie down into the Little Muddy River.

Keith was finished with the college and the community. In such a small place, he thought people would be friendlier. Instead, he found the opposite. No one had ever invited him to their home. He was alone living in the middle of nowhere. His wife was living and working in another state. He was miserable.

Even after several years at the college, Keith was still considered an outsider. His leaving would only confirm that impression. Looking out from the backside of his trailer, I did not doubt his sincerity. Keith had made his best effort. Like the 19th century, the land was still inhospitable. Like the trailers, like Dickson Hall, like Keith, neglect spanned as far as my eyes could see.

College Neglect and Abuse

The primary buildings at the college were in the same condition as the trailer park and Dickson Hall. The Veteran's Memorial at the school's entrance was collapsing on itself. The main building, Stevens Hall, was a disaster. The college's mailing address was P.O. Box 1326. It reminded me of a fake correspondence school.

Williston State had not changed in over forty years. Visitors and alums would proudly say: "Wow! The college looks the same as when I went to school," referencing the late 1960s. The compliment was like someone coming to your home for the first time in 40 years: "Wow! Your home looks the same as when I visited here 40 years ago."

The college was operating at a deficit. The finance staff was six months behind. Food services and the bookstore lost money. The baseball field project was $90,000 short, so construction had stopped.

Stevens Hall was filthy. Wireless systems were not updated because of asbestos in the ceilings. Flooring had not been updated because of asbestos under the vinyl. Dust came out of the vents. It clotted and adhered to the walls. The building had experienced zero renovation.

Offices were placed in random locations. Signage was out of date. Whether you wanted to go to the business office or the student office, you were ultimately going to arrive at the wrong place if you followed the signs.

Faculty members packed in three or four to an office. I visited a faculty "suite." Three people crammed into an oblong room. I asked: "How is everything?" Faye, a math instructor, said "Great." I scanned the room, nodded, and inquired: "And, why are the computer monitors on the floor?"

Apparently, the desks were built in the late sixties when the college did not have computers; the monitors did not fit. As Faye balanced the keyboard on her lap, she pointed down at the monitor and said: "So the best place is on the floor."

Looking around I noticed there was no ventilation. A little confused, I asked if there was ventilation in the office. Faye said no. I asked if that caused any problems. Silence. Another faculty member finally poked her head out of a cubicle and said: "We get headaches." I learned later that when the college ran short of office space, they built offices out of storage closets.

This was truly the North Dakota way, the North Dakota spirit. People suffered quietly. People were grateful for what they had. They certainly didn't believe they were entitled to anything more.

Even those with disabilities were undeserving. Disability services, like adult education, was not immune to the spirit of neglect. Located on the second floor of Stevens Hall, it was served by an elevator so small that one could see scuff marks left by wheelchairs attempting to squeeze in and out of the tiny compartment.

Matt, an economics instructor and the one staff member using a wheelchair also resided on the second floor. During a fire drill, I accompanied Matt from his office to the stairs. We looked at each other, and I could tell he did not want me to carry him down the stairs. "It's just a drill," he said. There was no other way I could move Matt down two flights of stairs and not risk his life. We were stuck. We ended up taking the elevator, the most dangerous way to get downstairs during a fire.

The college choral concert I attended was also on the second floor. I met a person using a wheelchair attempting to get into the elevator to attend the concert. I squeezed the wheelchair into the elevator. Once he was in the elevator, I ran up the stairs to assist his exit. This time, I was the one scratching the elevator door. That summer, I took the time to personally repaint both elevator doors.

The community had adapted to a culture tolerant of hardships. One could call this benign neglect, but benign neglect over decades is abuse. To be fair, I admired the stoicism. There was an innocence that was appealing. But the innocence was a double-edged sword. One side of the sword spelled trouble.

Whether the adult education trailer, the student residence hall or staff housing, I began to understand a community that suffered from much more than extreme isolation. I had heard of similar experiences in service projects I had been a part of in inner cities and in the Appalachian Mountains. But this was my first time living in a rural community in "America's Heartland." I had become a member of an abandoned, neglected and ultimately, battered community.

I was getting nervous. Joyce was battling a lawsuit alone in Washington with a newborn and a toddler, as well as two girls in grade school. I had a house to prepare for my family, and a million tasks awaited me at the college. I also knew Williston in no way resembled Joyce's dream of the Great Plains people. Like Keith, I was in trouble. I just hoped that when my family did arrive, we would be able to make things work.

Arriving three to six months before the boom did allow me to put some infrastructure into place. If I had arrived any later, I would have been in a world of hurt. Still, my family and I were in no way prepared for what was to come.

—

PRE-BOOM CHANGE

"Build too little, and they'll wind up with a city overrun by RV parks and unsafe living conditions. Build too much, and they could repeat the disastrous situation that arose in the 1980s when the last boom went bust. Back then, many cities were happy to help developers fill the housing void by building infrastructure for new homes in the hopes that the units would not only accommodate their new residents, but also generate property tax revenue. Then, almost overnight, oil prices fell. The industry pulled out, and the developers left town since they owed more in property taxes on undeveloped land than the value of the land itself. In Williston, the city took ownership of those developments – it eventually owned a quarter of the town – and was stuck with more than $25 million in debt on the infrastructure without a tax base to pay it off."[16]

—*Governing*, August, 2011

Once I accepted the job, Chancellor Goetz and the search consultant provided me a mandate for change. Maybe mandate is too strong. The consultant told me to replace the senior staff. This was not as easy as one would think.

Finding qualified people in sparsely populated, northwest North Dakota was like mining for gold. You had to know where to look, and you had to get lucky. Between the adult education building and paying for the student residence hall, I was not in a position to go mining for three new executive members on staff.

So I began with the Vice President for Academic Affairs. The VP's quiet disposition was quite in keeping with North Dakota's puritan mindset, but I needed cheerleaders on my leadership team. We worked out a six-month exit plan. She would be paid an additional six months and "consult." The End. Or so I thought.

Soon after our agreement, I received a visit from her husband. A large burly man, and owner an oil related business, he attempted to intimidate me. He talked about his standing in the community. He disclosed gifts he made to the technical programs. Bottom line: He wanted his wife back in her job.

I was aghast. I had never participated in this level of personal confrontation on the part of an employee relation. But if I was caught off guard by his visit, I was equally unbalanced at the chancellor's response when I shared the incident with him. Apparently, the husband had taken the four-hour drive to Bismarck to meet with the chancellor too.

In North Dakota, EVERYONE is accessible. This includes everyone from the Governor to the presidents of the research universities, to the chancellor, to me. As would become the norm, the personal element came into play even in a decision directed by my supervisor. The decision was not reversed, but in many instances, the personal touch could very well change the outcome.

To further my understanding of the college and its needs, I decided to meet with all staff individually. As there were just over one hundred staff members, it was doable. Employees were skeptical of my taking thirty minutes to meet with them, but the results were invaluable.

Moving ahead, I created a list of inexpensive, cosmetic facelifts. I would begin by changing the current environment. For every action I would take, there would be push back. But over time, I reasoned, the changes would make a difference. I just had to be diligent.

Carpet tiles were laid over the 47-year-old linoleum floors. A rumor circulated the president was stealing money to carpet the floors. Staff informed me that colleges in North Dakota did not have carpet. On later visits to other campuses, I noted North Dakota campuses did indeed have carpeted floors. Staff and students incorrectly assumed that other campuses were just like their campus. To save money, staff rarely traveled so they were not in a position to understand the differences or even the progress made by the other colleges.

The biggest challenge, however, was enrollment. The campus looked like a ghost town. There was no quick fix for the enrollment numbers, but I could improve the optics by moving classes with high enrollment to the first floor. When classes ended, the hallway was humming with students. The college looked busy (at least on the first floor), and the new energy created a buzz. The community was talking positively about the college.

With growing momentum in the community, I became a little bolder. The Veteran's Memorial at the college's front door was an eyesore. If the college was going to have a memorial, the college needed to maintain it properly. The finance office complained there were no dollars, but Terry came through, and the foundation footed the bill to restore the memorial.

The college replaced its P.O. Box with a street address. At Executive Cabinet, heavy discussion took place on whether the college could even get a physical address. When I told Cabinet I would take care of the matter myself, staff moved quickly. 1410 University Avenue replaced P.O. Box 1326.

We introduced an art classroom. The faculty was asked to purchase art supplies. They went online to IKEA and identified a list of furniture. Faculty had never spent money on furniture. IKEA online was the least expensive option they could find.

I envisioned a different experience. I was imagining a room that would inspire thinking that if an artist walked by, they would say: "Wow, I want to paint here." An IKEA-equipped classroom did not fit that vision.

Since the foundation was funding the project, faculty went back and purchased furniture from an art supply store. The faculty was so proud of the space that they threw an opening for the new classroom. There was a collective "Wow." A few thought it was extravagant. I was happy with the "Wow."

Student Services moved from multiple locations across campus into one easy-to-find space. The business office, also scattered across campus, collocated into one space. Food service, operated by a private vendor, had lost almost $100,000. That contract was terminated, and a manager was hired.

Williston State did not have a marketing department. When I asked about obtaining business cards, I learned people made their own. It was true. I counted at least seven different types of business cards (at least for those who had them).

By fall, the college had the beginning of a marketing office and a new website was under development. I contacted the college history professor's wife to write press releases for twenty dollars per press release. The sheer number of small improvements was making a noticeable difference.

Because of the changes, some faculty and staff decided it was time to leave the college. An auto instructor with a record of student grievances gave notice. An accounting instructor with a history of not showing up to work resigned. The director of financial aid quit when she was asked to work five days a week in the office versus three days in the office and two days from home.

The baseball field was finished. A dedication was held. Fall headcount was up 12%. But more importantly, Joyce and the children had finally made the move. The girls were enrolled in school. We were a family again. And at least for myself, Williston was starting to feel like home.

But in many ways, my job had just begun. There was no security on campus. Employees were woefully underpaid. There was a great deal left to do in a community that had settled for far too little for far too long.

Master Plan

What no one knew was that change would come regardless of my efforts. The college would be swept up in the oil boom. We would all have to learn to navigate through changes that would affect us at every level.

As luck would have it, Brad Bekkedahl, a city commissioner and a man of vision, told me that the college needed a master plan. Developing a master plan is an expensive process, and the college was in dire financial straits. My first emails from the vice chancellor for finance, Laura Glatt were not the customary "Hello" and "Welcome" emails. The emails looked more like those outsourced to a credit agency for collection purposes.

Brad, one of those rare government servants, one might even say a super volunteer, came up with the roughly $50,000 from the city's budget. Brad, a city commissioner, a dentist, a lieutenant colonel in the national guard, a board member on the national junior hockey league, and he still made time to visit his parents in the nursing home every evening. There were probably three people that made the city work, and Brad was one of them.

So, money in hand, the college went to work. The plan was loaded with lofty dreams. I had waited for this opportunity for nearly 50 years. I had not come to North Dakota to be the president of a trailer park. And Brad provided the right tools to get the college back on track.

By the end of my first year, I had removed four trailers from campus. I was on fire. I was ready to do the impossible. What I didn't know was that the boom would make everything both possible and impossible.

The price of oil was going up, and people remained skeptical. People had been burned in the last boom, and they were not prepared or interested in being burned again. The state, living off scarce resources for decades, was not about to abandon its hyper-conservative position by diverting resources to the northwest. Farmers were even less pleased with the oil gossip. "North Dakota's economy is based on agriculture," I heard time and time again.

But this boom would be on a scale comparable to the 1849 Gold Rush. Industry would invest billions of dollars in a four-county area. The state would invest billions in roads. The population of Williston would triple.

So how does one prepare for such an event? There were no textbooks or papers or instructions that addressed how to deal with an approaching tsunami. But armed with a master plan, we naively thought we were ready. No one could have predicted the size or the number of waves that followed.

Family Doubts

The story of my family's transition to an oil patch community was one I would see time and time again in Williston. The schools were overcrowded. There was no bus service. And a lack of daycare made it nearly impossible for Joyce to work away from home. Joyce turned into the children's chauffeur.

The children saw none of the Joyce's struggles. They were enjoying their move from the city to the country. In the city, the girls were small fish in a big pond. In Williston, the girls were big fish in a little pond. In the city, we all held hands as we dodged traffic. In the country, the girls ran through the prairie, threw rocks, crossed the street to see their friends, and enjoyed an unparalleled level of freedom. Our condo in Seattle had a great view but was small. In North Dakota, the girls played hide and seek in the house and spent a lot of time in the backyard's brick playhouse equipped with its own intercom system and electricity.

But Joyce had certainly not prepared for, or anticipated, the level of neglect experienced in this community. Joyce had enjoyed incredible freedom and success in the city. In Williston, Joyce was expected to play the role of the president's wife. People constantly referred to her as Mrs. Nadolny (not her last name). The conversation always revolved around me and the many changes taking place at the college. Joyce felt invisible.

Suffice to say, she was not in her element. Joyce did not earn her bachelor's from Harvard and J.D. at NYU, or become the chief administrative officer at one of Seattle's IT companies to have no identity other than as the president's wife. It was not one of her dreams growing up. It was certainly not on her list of career aspirations. Joyce felt like she had taken an unexpected, and unpleasant, step back in time.

Joyce's good faith efforts met with surprise and even annoyance. Conversant in French, Spanish, Chinese, and Japanese and having run a business for almost ten years in addition to being an accomplished lawyer and successful company executive and with a very strong network back home, she could not find an executive job locally.

So she volunteered to teach Spanish to toddlers at the local Parks and Recreation for a period to introduce our community to the fun of learning a second language. During open gym time, little children gravitated to her corner where she sang songs and played games. A few weeks later, she was unceremoniously stopped by one of the Parks staff from entering. She was told she could not continue to come back. Multiple families had complained their children were being exposed to Spanish without their consent. It seems that because the activity was taking place in a large open area, and Joyce's program was magnetizing enough that the families could not stop their children from participating. Parks chose to accommodate their fears by removing Joyce. Joyce's efforts were foreign, her brand of volunteerism not recognizable. Realization dawned: Joyce was not with her people. Her efforts were not appreciated. She felt even more isolated in this small community for which she had so much hope.

The first winter added to the isolation. It was fierce, and it was cold. Roads were dangerous. Back in Williston, Joyce found herself stranded at home and without friends. She missed Seattle, her access to diverse foods, and generous-hearted friends who would call and visit. While I was attending to the college and community, she was suffocating.

I discussed my wife's situation with the president of the University of North Dakota. He expressed the same frustration with his wife's situation: "Marsha works a full-time job but gets treated like a glorified volunteer."

That summer, a scandal broke out concerning the wife of the president of North Dakota State University. She was being paid $50,000 a year by the university's foundation. Although paying the spouse of the president was a national trend in universities at least in partial recognition of the time and effort expended by the spouse, North Dakota was not ready to pay for the work being provided for free by the wives of North Dakota's college presidents. The president of North Dakota State University eventually resigned under the pressure, and Joyce began to rethink her decision to come to North Dakota.

Chapter 3
OIL PATCH PRESIDENT[17]

"As long as you have something to look forward to, a little glimmer of hope, you can move on. But this just drained everything out of us."

— Councilman Jay LaFont of Grand Isle, Louisiana
on the 2010 BP Gulf Oil Spill

A BAD START

By the end of my first full year, my confidence was growing. But the BP Gulf Oil Spill in 2010 served as a wake-up call. I was starting to feel first-hand the impact of Williston's own impending oil spill. Employees began leaving for oil jobs. Finding replacements, already difficult, was becoming impossible. Rising rents were taking a toll. Life was still manageable, but the signs were everywhere. Oil activity was increasing.

It was also the first summer I would spend with my family in Williston. Fortunately, the United States Air Force, probably at the instigation of oil companies, understood the severity of the Williston mosquito problem. Multiple flights were made over Williston to spray away the pests, eliminating what has been a scourge for nearly three centuries.

I had given up vacation time the previous summer to totally immerse myself in the college, and the sacrifices were paying off. With a string of successes, my feet on the ground, it was time to take a vacation. Joyce's family was in New York, and I needed to get Joyce "out of Dodge." Joyce had not made many friends and like Keith was growing more and more isolated.

Unfortunately, taking time off in an oil boom economy has consequences. As time would tell, any leave on my part would lead to some emergency at the college. I didn't know it, but I had strapped myself into a rollercoaster that would run for six years.

It only took one short newspaper article followed by a summons to the Governor's Office to remind me of what really matters in North Dakota. Not two days into a family visit with my in-laws in New York, I received a short text: "Governor trying to reach you."

Of course, every little boy dreams of getting a call from the Governor: "Congratulations on saving that puppy's life." Or, "The Governor would like to award you the Medal of Honor for pulling that baby out of the fire." But this was not to be one of those conversations. Only on the job for one year, I had a very bad feeling, like a boy being called to the principal's office.

On July 4, 2010, a day before I left on vacation, the *Williston Herald* published my opinion piece. I compared northwest North Dakota's situation to the recent Gulf Spill in New Orleans. I predicted that a similar tragedy would take place in rural Northwestern North Dakota if the state did not start investing in the area's infrastructure.

I had begun to see the emergence of the oil boom. I had already started to anticipate its impact on the community. Although prophetic, my words were ill-timed. In a small town, with a small hometown newspaper, the power held by the oil industry was about to spill over me like a tipped drum of "Texas tea."

My column was short on words and seemed simple, if not constructive:

> An oil spill can take place in a variety of ways. In the gulf region, the spill begins on water and eventually reaches land. In the northwest portion of North Dakota, it starts with man camps, unaffordable

housing, insufficient infrastructure, and dangerous roads. The gulf spill comes with a 20 billion dollar fund with the idea if more is needed, more will come. The North Dakota spill comes with new jobs, a promise of wealth for a few, and, if anything like the last boom, a community left with both a depleted infrastructure and significantly in debt.

The nation, the state has made a decision to invest in tragedy, the gulf spill. The nation, the state appears to be ignoring an incredible opportunity, which has the appearance and could very well be a tragedy for the people of Northwest North Dakota. On a daily basis, mostly young men are getting off the train, having traveled from across the country from a state ravaged by the economy, for the promise of a job. The job is indeed here, but finding a hotel is improbable, and decent housing for the majority is impossible.

When they come for training on campus, they find themselves sardined into a building that looks more like a tough shed than a training center. And good luck at getting into one of the two bathrooms. And in the past several months, we have people walking into campus to find out the minimum number of credits so that they can take advantage of our housing. Well, as of June, our housing is full.

With all the opportunity, some of these tragedies are already starting to set in to our community. Our building costs are soaring. Our capital projects, on some days, are nightmares. How much can a College downsize and still attempt to fulfill its mission? Faculty and staff are currently seeing their rents skyrocket. How much longer can they afford to live here? And how can we get quality faculty for our students? Where can new faculty live? And if they live outside of our area, how safe are our roads?

If there is a time to invest in the western part of the state, to increase our state tax base, to grow new communities, to build a community rather than to deplete it of its resources, the time is now. The petroleum industry, state and national officials have a tremendous opportunity to respond to opportunity, not just tragedy. And hopefully, they will act before this becomes a tragedy for the next generation, the northwest region of North Dakota, and the state of North Dakota.

I was greeted by Governor Hoeven (now U.S. Senator Hoeven) and the Governor's chief of staff, Ron Rauschenberger. Governor Hoeven's message was simple. The oil industry is the lifeblood of the state. As it kicks into gear, the state must do everything it can to support this significant economic opportunity.

Governor Hoeven was not a stranger to Williston State College, nor was it the first time I had met him. He had come to the college for the dedication of the new TrainND building. The facility, built to train workers in the oil industry, would be overwhelmed in less than a year.

At the dedication, Governor Hoeven was excited. He understood the potential wealth of the oil in the Bakken formation. He also knew I was a first-time president. I would only get my hands slapped this time. Governor Hoeven's message was positive, and we all smiled. But the warning was clear. I had stepped over a line.

I had come to North Dakota to survive a recession and make a success of the college, and within my first year, I nearly lost my livelihood and my dreams. For the first time, I realized I was an oil patch president. I needed to learn everything I could about the oil industry. Oil was here to stay, like a river that changed course and went through town. I could not move the river, I could not change its direction, but at the very least, I could take advantage of the changes in current. I could leverage new training programs as well as provide a quality of life component to the College that was sorely missing in the community. Williston was making the big move from small town to small city in a short period of time. I was in a position to make that transition easier.

The small town was already charting new territory, breaking new records. In 2005, 14 million barrels of oil was projected. In 2008, two billion barrels of oil was projected. In 2010, the number nearly doubled again to four billion. Williston eclipsed Grand Forks, North Dakota's second largest city, in retail sales. This oil boom was a gusher.

Sabotage

"Man camps provide temporary employee housing to oilfield workers and have increased in number due to influxes in population coupled with housing shortages in remote drilling areas. Man camp accommodations can range from recreational vehicles and barracks-style modulars to luxury lodge accommodations. These camps are intended to be self-sufficient 'communities.' The camps not only provide shelter for the transient oilfield worker but also dining, laundry, and recreational facilities."

—OGFI, What the Frac is an Oil Camp[18]

The fact remained that Williston was in the epicenter of what was quickly becoming a jungle. And the jungle was far more treacherous than anything Williston had experienced before. The city, scant on resources and people, would sabotage itself repeatedly. As an example, the opening of two new parks should have been celebratory events. But it was hard to celebrate the new parks with the city's concurrent approval of a strip club and a man camp.

The first park cost $1.6 million and was meant to beautify the train station, which served as the entrance for most Williston visitors. But at the same time the park was being built, the city provided a license for a second strip club, Heartbreakers. Whispers and Heartbreakers, located almost next to each other, were across the street from the new park. People getting off the train could look straight ahead and see Williston's Main Street. Looking right, they would see a beautiful railroad park. Looking left, they would see two strip clubs. Welcome to Williston.

A few months later, the Park District opened Davidson Park, the largest continuous playground in the state. Built on community donations, the $660,000 park was developed to celebrate the oil community, its slide towers in the shape of oil derricks. Just one week after the opening, the city council licensed an outdoor man camp adjacent to Davidson Park. Locals called the man camp "Tent City," as more than 30 tents popped up across the grounds. Concerns arose over potential child predators next to a children's park.

The opening of the man camp right after the opening of the playground was incredulous, but it didn't seem like news to those able to do something about it. The Chamber of Commerce attempted a soft sell on the camps, but the residents around Tent City would have nothing to do with the pretense. It took an increasing number of complaints involving alcohol to finally close it. Surprisingly, the press was nowhere to be found. Oil had become the big news. The opportunities brought by the oil industry allowed most people to turn a blind eye.

—

THE MINNESOTA WHEAT KING

"There's various kind of oil aflout, Cod-liver, Sweet;
Which tend to make a sick man well,
and set him on his feet,
But our's a curious feat performs:

We just a *well* obtain,
And set the people crazy with "Oil on the brain."

—Oil on the Brain, 19th Century Song

Now that I had met the Governor twice, it was time to take the bull by the horns. It was time to discuss the needs of an oil patch college. I requested a meeting.

Terry Olson and I made the trip to the Governor's Office. Terry was admired and liked across the state, and it seemed that between the two of us, we had a shot at capturing the governor's attention. The Governor was joined by Lieutenant Governor Jack Dalrymple. Later, when Governor Hoeven won his bid to the US Senate, Jack Dalrymple would succeed him.

The meeting did not go as hoped. While Governor Hoeven praised the college's efforts in workforce development, our plans for the campus to resemble a collegiate environment were considered extravagant. What everyone wanted in Williston was a premiere technical school.

The state, however, was not willing to pay the costs associated with high-tech credit training. Seven hours away from Williston, in the heart of what could truly be called the diesel capitol of the country, the president of North Dakota State College of Science (NDSCS) had already complained that Williston's diesel program was a duplicate and should be closed. Colleges in the east were concerned about their enrollment. Williston State was another worry to schools with a history of diminishing enrollments.

I was dejected. The community's vision of a comprehensive college in isolated northwest North Dakota was just that… a dream. Until, as I was about the leave, the lieutenant governor tapped me on the shoulder.

I am not sure what Williston would have done without Governor Dalyrmple. At the time, Lieutenant Governor Dalrymple, came from generations of North Dakota wheat farmers. His family was an agricultural force in North Dakota for the past two centuries. His great grandfather, a Yale law school graduate in 1856, was known as the "Minnesota Wheat King." Also a graduate of Yale, Jack Dalrymple had a more expansive vision of North Dakota. He tapped me on the shoulder and said: "Don't give up on that plan. Stick to it." And he gave me a wink.

The wink was a kick-start. Several months later, in a meeting with representatives from Hess Corporation, both the Governor and Lieutenant Governor brought up Williston State's plan. They told the Hess consultants that Williston State was in the best position to confront inflationary forces by meeting the demands of the growing oil industry. Hess did not bite. They were not about to invest in capital projects.

Hess would invest in education, but they were only willing to teach people, as one consultant put it: "how to ride the bike." It didn't seem to matter to the Hess consultants that Williston had few bikes to offer and most of those bikes should not have been on the road. They were clear; they would not be providing any infrastructure dollars. As children took classes in renovated FEMA trailers, Hess cast a blind eye, building virtual education silos to bolster their name and their oil claim in the state.

The meeting was not a total loss. The college now had the ear of the governor and the lieutenant governor. As events unfolded and these men advanced, both became powerful allies.

Inflation

Williston was spiraling from wage inflation to housing inflation to the spiking cost of goods and services. CNN reported on Williston strippers earning higher wages than strippers in Las Vegas. CNN even did a story on one of the college's English professors entitled: "My Students Make Twice My Salary."

The least likely people were being affected by the boom. Both college's librarians left during my second year at the college. The first left to work for an oil company. The second librarian left because of escalating rents. No position was immune to the promise of riches being made by an increasing number of oil-related businesses, nor their growing appetites for a small but highly sought after pool of workers.

The legislative process was not set up to react to the inflationary forces overwhelming Williston. North Dakota's legislature did not meet annually, and the last biennium funding did not allow the college to increase salaries at any level to help college employees stay at the college or in their homes. There was no one at the legislature to even make a request for the money we needed to keep up. Many of the college's projects faltered or just stopped.

The science project was reduced in scope even before it went out to bid. The lowest bid came in $200,000 over budget. Even with the additional cuts, the lowest bid was now an astounding $300,000 over budget, or $100,000 higher than the last bid even with the cuts. There was nothing to do but shelve the science project. Lance was at wit's end. Another legislative request would have to be made but we would have to wait.

The career and technical education building was a disaster. The liberal arts faculty member in charge of the project was very understandably out of his depth. Costs could not be maintained. The builder had taken on too many projects and had at least one pending lawsuit. The planned multi-story career and technical education facility had to be scaled down to a one-story building.

The residence hall was downsized from 220 beds to 171 beds. It was debatable whether 80% occupancy would cover the bond payment, so I had a conference room placed on the top level. As a relative sky scraper in our small town, the fourth floor conference room offered stunning views showcasing the area's natural beauty. The hope was that conference services would supplement housing revenue by hosting events over the summer and operate as buffer for the ups and downs of student housing. Community members have used the conference floor for wedding receptions and other high-end events, bringing people and rave reviews in to our campus from all over the state. With employee turnover occurring annually in both housing and conference services, the idea, though sound, had to remain more "opportunity" than fully-realized reality.

With the college struggling financially, the vice president for business affairs took a more lucrative position with an oil company. A mad quest for a replacement took place as I assumed control of the business office. Given the college's poor fiscal position and my lacking a finance background, the situation looked bleak.

High-level finance people were at a premium, so recruiting a vice president for business affairs was a priority. Two of the three candidates that applied did so at my invitation. Technically, staff is not allowed to recruit college employees as there could be the perception of preferential treatment. A whistleblower complaint was filed against me for actively recruiting employees. Everything had changed in Williston. To hire, one had to recruit. One had to recruit actively, and it would still not be enough.

Only three people applied. Two of the candidates I personally recruited. The highest rated applicant for the position was out of state. The position was offered and the candidate counter-offered with a higher salary. I accepted. The applicant then counter-offered again, demanding a housing package. I declined. The candidate walked.

The position was then offered to the local bank loan officer who, fortunately, accepted. If he had not, an offer for the vice president of business affairs would have been made to the third candidate who did not have a college degree. The college was clearly in a bind.

We were not the only organization on the hunt for employees. Every Monday, Wednesday and Friday, a group of community leaders (all men) played basketball on the college's old gym court. The group went by the name of "Noonball." As the college was nearly broke, I brought a motion to the executive cabinet to charge the group a nominal fee for the use of the gym. Terry pulled me aside and explained that several of the Noonballers were managers of major oil companies. More importantly, most of the players were significant donors to the foundation. Needless to say, I pulled my request.

Not three weeks later, I lost two employees to the Noonballers. Before and after Noonball, the managers would chat up college employees looking for new recruits. I made a personal visit to the gym. I made it clear to the men that if I lost another employee, I would end Noonball. Employee attrition, at least from this group, stopped.

Safety

Campus security had also emerged as a serious and potentially disastrous concern. Williston's police were short-staffed and stretched dangerously thin. State emergency funding was requested based on a local security company's rate of $28 per hour. For the first time in the college's history, the college would have limited evening security. Just after the state approved the request, the security company increased their rate from $28 per hour to $35 per hour. The hours had to be reduced.

The security firm contracted by the college had more on their plate than they could handle. Vagrants on campus were a common occurrence. A man was found living in a cargo trailer on the south edge of the residence hall construction site with his trailer plugged into the exterior of the residence hall for power. Female residents in Abramson Hall were concerned and reported the man. It would be the first of many such occurrences.

Neighborhoods were changing; the college was changing. People waited in long lines at bars, banks, restaurants, and retail stores. Increased traffic congestion and the large number of 18-wheelers caused additional stress for people getting to the grocery store or to their place of work. When one did get to the grocery store, many of the aisles were empty. Mancamps, eager to feed their residents, would clean out the stores of major foodstuffs. Even the architects complained, telling me that on a trip to Arby's, they were informed the fast food franchise had run out of roast beef.

No one was really sure what to make of it. For the first time, long-time residents did not feel safe. New college employees, arriving with spouses hired in the oil field, were also having a difficult time. And, as in the case of Glen and Pam Gardner, hope was descending into tragedy.

Glen Gardner

> "The life of man, solitary, poor, nasty, brutish, and short."
> —Thomas Hobbes, *The Leviathan*

Dr. Pam Gardner was the college's first oil field employee catch. Pam's husband had been offered a job with Key Energy. Pam was offered the position of Dean.

Dr. Gardner brought top-level personal and professional experience. She and her husband had two children and seven grand-children. She had successfully acquired over $10 million in grants and appropriations at her previous university. She was a breath of fresh air in a college that was suffocating.

A recipient of numerous leadership awards, Dr. Gardner received the prestigious International Futures Award for Exceptional and Innovative Leadership in Continuing Higher Education. She held a doctorate in Educational Leadership from Brigham Young University. When asked why she decided to come to Williston State College, she replied with the politically correct response: "Because of the exceptional leadership and passion for education I see here. The college is poised for greatness. I'm excited to have a role in its metamorphosis."

I did not know Dr. Gardner's family story until I met her husband. A complaint came to the president's office about an older man "squatting" in the bookstore sitting area. The number of transients coming into the college was on an uptick. The person in question had come each day for the past three days. As the college did not have daytime security, I checked out the matter myself.

A small but sturdy man wearing boots, jeans and a flannel shirt was watching TV. I walked up and introduced myself. To my surprise, the man introduced himself as Dr. Gardner's husband, Glen.

Glen was born in Ohio but grew up in Utah. Glen and Pam were high school sweethearts. He worked at Boeing helping build the first 747s. He became a journeyman and contractor, and later he became a businessman in Utah. With the recession, his fortunes changed. He lost his company and they left their million-dollar home.

I was struck by the kindness and intelligence in Glen's voice. I discovered later that he was a high priest in the LDS Church. Williston, for Glen and so many others, was a ticket to a new future.

Glen asked me if it was okay to continue to visit the lounge. He was completing his paperwork for his new job as a construction manager at Key Energy. I let him know he could use the lounge anytime. We exchanged a few pleasantries, and I left.

I saw Glen a week later, the night before he died. Our vice president for instruction held a dinner at her home to welcome Pam and Glen to town. Pam had been at the college for three months. Glenn had only recently arrived. She wanted to make sure we retained this dynamic couple. We had an enjoyable dinner which my wife would later note seemed like it could be a turning point for her, chatting with several interesting people over dinner at a local family's home.

The day after the dinner, however, Glen went to the hospital to take a routine stress test for his new job. During the stress test, Glen suddenly and inexplicably died. I went to the hospital that day and sat with Pam and some of the elders of her church.

On my return to campus, I stopped at a grocery store and purchased some food. Pam and Glen were residents in what was now one of the new trailers I had placed on campus. As president, I had access to all the trailers and asked for permission to enter as I wanted to stock Pam's refrigerator with nourishing food and drinks.

When I opened the door to the single wide mobile, I was greeted by a grand piano. Not any grand piano. One of Liberace's grand pianos. Colorfully ornate, the piano was extravagant. I felt like I had stepped into a sort of twilight zone or a back-alley Vegas show club.

Glen's death was a shock. Finding a Liberace grand piano in a single-wide trailer was both overwhelming and somehow deeply disturbing. I learned later from Pam that the piano was her last reminder of all the things they once had. With everything that was taken away from them, she was not going to give up her passion for music and her treasured piano.

After Glen's death, I thought Pam would immediately leave the college, but she stayed another year before returning home to Utah. Like so many that came to Williston hoping for a new start, Pam left with a tragic loss. And with so many new employees coming to the college, their times were often brief, filled with both heartwarming and heart wrenching experiences.

It was also the first time I became aware that Keith's feeling of isolation had become Joyce's own experience of the community. Joyce was shocked to be invited to the dinner with Glen as she had been living in Williston for over a year and this was one of her first invitations to dinner at a family home. While I ran around town playing hero, Joyce was left alone to care for a one-year-old, three-year-old, ten-year-old and twelve-year-old. In a community that prided itself on being kind, Joyce only saw loneliness and isolation. She was still smarting from being asked to leave the parks and recreation center. She asked me, "What if I had been volunteering to make Christmas crafts in the room? Do you think multiple families here would have complained? And do you think parks would have responded by eliminating my program? What would you have done, Mr. President?" It was a rhetorical question. She already knew my answer. But that was not the reality of our community at that time. Still, she was determined to stay positive. How much longer she could maintain a happy face was left to be seen.

—

HIGH RISK

> "North Dakota is booming. Its unemployment rate is the lowest in the country, 3.7 per cent, and so many people have moved there for jobs that last year local officials declared a housing crisis. The new workers have been drawn by the Williston Basin, in the western part of the state, which holds the largest accumulation of oil identified in North America since 1968, when the Prudhoe Bay field was found, on the North Slope of Alaska. Oil companies have booked motels within two hours' drive for a year in advance; last summer, relocated workers converted the lawn of a town park into a tent city."
>
> —"Kuwait on the Prairie," *The New Yorker*, April 20, 2011[19]

The boom began to show its teeth. Employee turnover picked up steam and contributed to steep declines in staff morale. The college struggled with hyperinflation, childcare, and basic health care services. I called Representative Skarphol. I was, in all honesty, overwhelmed. I realized I was no longer operating in a small community or for that matter in a small college. His response was both quick and supportive. He directed me to write up exactly what the college required. He would personally take my request to the legislature.

High Risk

A report came out assessing the health and well-being of the university system's eleven institutions. Williston State was identified as high risk, making it easier for me to write up my case for Representative Skarphol. Even so, the focus of the State Board continued to be on issues related to the University of North Dakota's Fighting Sioux logo. No attention was paid to the college.

Williston State was the only college in the university system's report identified as a safety risk. Williston police calls increased

250%. Traffic accidents doubled. From 2010 to 2014, the population of Williston would grow an astounding 67%. We were only in the middle of that growth, and no one really believed it would continue at that same unadulterated pace. No one believed it could.

Williston area wages were now the highest in the state. Wages increased 20 percent over the previous year and were up 80 percent since 2006. The average salary in the Fourth Quarter of 2011 was $77,272, a ten percent increase in three months. Wages were sky-rocketing.

Staff turnover was at 30 percent. The college was struggling. Employee housing in the current climate was increasingly unaffordable. Finding someone to do repairs was difficult if not impossible. If someone was found, the costs were outrageous. Higher costs and lack of overall housing meant sharp rent increases. The college was not immune. College employees living on campus saw their rents increase.

Dr. Gardner identified the concern a couple of months before she resigned: "I've recently become aware of a 25% increase in the rent for those of us living in college-owned trailers. In all honesty, that increase seems excessive in light of the proposed salary increase of only 3%." Nothing could be done to mitigate this unfortunate situation. Costs were spiraling. Housing was losing money.

Restaurants closed because of a lack of employees. Long lines impacted all services. The school district did not have buses, so parents had to arrange transportation. With little childcare available, a large segment of the population found their work situations compromised as they had to stay home from work or bring their children to work.

The town appeared to be spiraling out of control. The city looked worse than when I arrived. While private industry was investing billions in northwest North Dakota, the State Board was nowhere to be seen. Williston State continued to remain off the radar of a State Board still preoccupied with the Fighting Sioux controversy.

Moving Forward

There was no stopping the boom. There was only the opportunity to try to take advantage of the new terrain. Whether it was working at Walmart for $17 an hour, waiting tables for $25 an hour, or driving a truck for $80,000 a year, people were coming from across the country for high-paying jobs. On our shopping trips to Walmart, my two oldest daughters, Sophia and Kiana, would count the number of different states they would see on cars license plates. While driving through the state Capitol, Sophia asked me why all the license plates were the same. Her only reality had been living in a town where the clear majority of people were from out of state.

The college made the most out of the newfound opportunities. Williston State College had a new seal, a new logo, and a new website. A college hockey team and a women's fastpitch softball team were approved. The two sports brought excitement to a community in desperate need of an energy boost, so regardless of the cost (once again the foundation would foot the bill), the sports were approved with hockey beginning its first season just eight months later.

In anticipation of the next legislative session, the college hired Representative Patrick Hatlestad to be the new Career and Technical Education Director. Hatlestad had career experience with the Williston School District, and it was hoped he could mend bridges with several of the school districts. At the very least, Hatlestad could be of significant support to the college in the coming session. The thought was correct, but not the outcome.

Hatlestad was not only powerless in the legislature, but he was the quintessential curmudgeon. Hatlestad confirmed the monopoly on power held by a few legislators. Hatlestad had zero power and zero influence. The college would have to move forward despite him.

High-Risk President

My family was now in crisis. Joyce was not adjusting to the challenges of Williston, and I was little if any help. I left for work at

6:00 a.m. and tried to come home by 6:00 p.m. but evening events such as college sporting events and lectures were also commonplace in addition to dinner meetings with other local leaders.

Meanwhile, the vast majority of university system meetings took place four to seven hours away from Williston. Car travel was the only means of transportation. I woke up at 2 a.m. one time to drive to Fargo for one of the meetings, seven hours to the eastern side of the state. I participated in meetings all day as well as a dinner. I then drove home the seven hours arriving around 2 a.m. the next day. The travel demands were exhaustive. There was no way I could maintain the level of travel required without staying the night. So instead of marathon travel, I ended up attending the various state wide meetings, staying away from home, sometimes several nights in a row.

The lack of diversity in Williston was an additional stress. I remember how excited Joyce had become when she saw that a "Leland Tong" was on my interview committee. Leland was not Asian but Norwegian. When Corey Fong, the state tax commissioner came over for dinner, we made the same mistake again: Norwegian, not Asian. In conversations with people, Joyce was mistakenly labeled to me as Native American or Mexican American. She was called "you people."

On my arrival in Williston, I met a custodian who introduced himself as Whitey. "Whitey" was one of two employees of color on campus. It would have been dreadfully awkward to call him "Whitey." As president, I thought I would dodge controversy and just take a more formal approach. I asked him for his full name. He replied: "Darryl Whitecloud." I said: "Darryl, it is a pleasure meeting you." Darryl responded: "Please, I prefer for people to call me Whitey." When in Rome... Whitey it is.

I had become alarmed over safety in our once very secure neighborhood. I thought about not allowing our children to walk to and from school, just two blocks down the street. The neighborhood was becoming increasingly unsafe. On a Sunday morning, a drunk oil worker hit a tree a half a block from our house. He continued to drive until he pulled over in front of our house. He could not open his door due to the damage he incurred from hitting the tree, so he rolled down his window, climbed out of the car and immediately took off between our house and the neighbors'. A police car quickly pulled into our driveway, and the police officer went off in pursuit.

If this were an isolated incident, it would have been manageable. But strange men following my daughters after school, comments in grocery stores, and larger and larger trucks driven by men with very high testosterone levels was wearing. Trying to put a good spin on the community to both my employees and Joyce was no longer working.

Childcare was impossible to find, so Joyce was unable to seek a full-time position as an attorney. Even the one semester she spent teaching a public speaking class, she had to bring Julia and Emma to class because child care would consistently cancel last minute or not show up. Joyce with no professional life and me with my primary focus on the college rather than my family, friction in the family only increased.

Still the eternal optimist, Joyce offered to host a dinner party at our home to participate in an international virtual food and art show ("Serve and Project") that was taking place online. The date was around Chinese New Year's. Joyce thought it would be a way to support her artist friend while making new friends. Joyce spent two days preparing the food for twelve people. Unaccustomed to Chinese food (one person even admitted he did not eat vegetables), the food remained largely uneaten. The dinner fell flat.

I could not abandon the community but, unbeknownst to me, I had abandoned my wife and children through my frequent absences from home. As the job placed increasing demands, Joyce felt more and more alone. January became a tipping point.

Joyce began the year in Seattle with all four daughters. I remained in Williston working. She came back to Williston so we could celebrate Emma's second birthday party. She left again to

New Jersey to celebrate her dad's 80th birthday, which I was unable to attend because of work.

Joyce now found herself in a continuous loop of packing and unpacking, as the trips back and forth to Seattle became more frequent for her. I myself never returned to Seattle in the seven years that I lived in Williston. I was focused on our local community and left Seattle and ultimately Joyce, largely behind.

I think Joyce wanted my help to be understood and to make friends and alliances. But because of my position and the context that had been indelibly set in the community and state, i.e., that recognizing one's wife could result in damaged public image and even disciplinary action and termination, I did not step forward, which I am sure only served to compound Joyce's sense of isolation.

The warning signs were clear, but I was too busy to pay attention. While I was trying to keep a college together, my family was falling apart.

Chapter 4
A SERIES OF UNFORTUNATE EVENTS

With oil back at $100, Hamm is sitting pretty with the biggest holding in the Bakken and set to invest $1 billion there this year in his quest to prove that it is not just one of the biggest oil fields in the United States, but in the whole world. "Out of all the oil plays in the U.S., there's just one Bakken," Hamm says. "It towers above everything else."

—*Forbes*, June 27, 2011[20]

DISASTERS

Senator Stan Lyson brought Representative Sukkot, Representative Hatlestad, and Terry Olson to my office for a meeting. Lyson had served in the Williston police force for fifteen years until his retirement as sheriff. Also, a veteran, he served at least one tour of duty in Vietnam as a sniper. A tall, imposing man, he was a force of nature.

The power Senator Lyson wielded in the legislature was by sheer personality. He was not in the inner circle, but he was not afraid to make demands when needed. He had the exterior of an ex-sniper but inside beat the heart of a teddy bear.

Senator Lyson was his usual direct self. He wanted the college and the foundation to take over the city's Department of Motor

Vehicles (DMV). "The college is the only entity in Williston with the capacity to do it," he pushed.

State law required the Department of Transportation to outsource the DMV. The Chamber of Commerce was currently running the department, which served about 2,000 people with two million dollars in revenue. Overwhelmed with employee turnover in the Chamber office, they couldn't hire DMV staffing given the high wages and the sheer number of open jobs in the community. The DMV was closed more often than open. The Chamber gave notice. They were getting out of the DMV business.

Terry and I looked at each other and smiled. We were completely in sync. We would support the Department of Transportation and gain a friend on the Governor's staff (the Director for Transportation). We would earn some gold stars from our legislators in advance of the legislative session.

To further benefit the college, we would lease a part of the new Tech Building and create another cash asset. And maybe... just maybe... this could help our staffing concerns. DMV employees doing a good job could advance into college positions. All wishful thinking.

Within a week, we signed a contract and were working directly with the state's Director of Transportation. Within two months, the DMV, under the umbrella of the foundation, was operational. The college's director of small business development would manage the facility while HR and the finance office would provide support.

By the end of its first year of operation, the DMV increased its service from 2,000 people to just over 50,000 people. Revenue went from two million dollars annually to just over $12 million, and once again, DMV staff could not keep pace.

The college experienced higher turnover in the DMV than anywhere else in the college. The ten dollar per hour positions offered by the Chamber turned into over $40,000 per year plus benefits jobs. Even with the enormous increase in pay, the DMV could not retain employees, and the foundation was losing money.

Complaints came in daily from staff about the character and attitude of DMV customers. The DMV had holes in the wall from customers butting their heads. Security was a concern. The college lost a secretary working in the Tech Building in which DMV was housed. She, like many others, was afraid of the small percentage of DMV clientele that made life miserable for everyone.

Williston State succeeded in making friends with the Department of Transportation. The college stepped in when others could not. But at what cost? The college was carrying another workload. The DMV was turning into a disaster. But it was to be the year of disasters. 2011 had all the signs of an apocalypse.

Natural Disasters

A series of natural disasters began when Williston received a record 107.2 inches of snowfall, which shattered the previous record by 12.5 inches. When I came home from work, it seemed like all I was doing was shoveling snow. The snow was so heavy my neighbor hired a truck to move snow off his property so he could continue to shovel his drive. I purchased mini shovels for Emma and Julia, who used them as an excuse to play in the snow.

In late April, a freak snowstorm shut down the city for several days. It was the worst storm in anyone's memory. Roads were icy. Hundreds of trees brought down power lines.

Williston State was one of two colleges in the state without a backup generator. When an early spring snow storm hit, students were stuck in the residence hall with neither power nor heat. Getting in and out of town was dangerous. Long lines formed at the few open gas stations. Supermarkets remained open but lost everything in their refrigeration and freezing units. And it was only the beginning.

Kokusai Junior College

In order to provide Williston State students with opportunities for international cultural exchange, I began writing to colleges around the world, looking for a sister college relationship. Japan held especially excellent promise because it is a first-world country with first-class transportation and safety and Joyce, who had lived in Japan, speaks Japanese. So with great fanfare and largely because of Joyce's (volunteer) assistance, Williston State established a sister college relationship with a wonderful college in Tokyo, Kokusai Junior College, in 2010.

On April 7, 2011, Kokusai Junior College, Williston's sister college in Japan, had to shut down temporarily due to the "Great Sendi," a magnitude 9.0 earthquake, one of the most powerful in history. The earthquake and resulting tsunamis were felt as far south as Beijing and as far west as both Oregon and California. 230,000 people lost their homes. Over 15,000 people died, including family members of students at Kokusai.

The northeastern Japanese earthquake triggered massive tsunami waves. Tsunami waves as high as 33 feet, clocked at speeds as high as 500 mph, went as far inland as six miles. Tsunami warnings were triggered as far as the Pacific basin with nine-foot waves striking Oregon and California.

The waves devastated major Japanese coastal areas. Three nuclear reactors went through level 7 meltdowns, and residents within twelve miles of Fukushima Daiichi Nuclear Power Plant were evacuated. Initial cost estimates ranged from $14.5 billion to $183 billion. It became the costliest natural disaster in history. Some estimates are now as high at $300 billion.

Kokusai students and staff stressed over potential exposure to radiation. Energy conservation measures were put into place at the high point of Japan's oppressive summer. When Kokusai reopened in the heat of the blistering summer, thermostats could only be set at 83 degrees or higher to conserve energy.

So far away, Williston State could do nothing to help its sister college beyond sending encouraging words of support. But being 5,589 miles away, the earthquake added another concern as college faculty and staff worried about the safety of the many friends they had made through the partnership. But a natural disaster would strike much closer to home.

Minot Flood

Minot, North Dakota, at least in 2011, was Williston's shopping ground. Minot, lying on the Souris River, was 50 miles south of Canada and just over 120 miles east of Williston. Minot was settled in 1886 during the construction of the Great Northern Railway, and as a result of spectacular growth in 20th century earned the nickname "the Magic City."

Minot successfully marketed itself at the expense of Williston. Minot, an agricultural hub as well as home to an Air Force Base, called itself the gateway to the energy-rich Bakken region. Like many North Dakota cities, it was desperately trying to cash in on northwest North Dakota's oil boom, even though it was not at the center of it.

The quality of life in Williston was poor, so oil companies placed their management offices two hours away from the oil fields in places like Dickinson and Minot, which had the amenities Williston lacked. Over time, the strategy weakened. Williston would slowly improve its quality of life and in some cases even outpaced both Dickinson and Minot. Oil companies became tired of the two plus hour commutes from either Dickinson or Minot to the Oil Patch. When the boom turned to bust, the first offices to close would be those farthest from the action.

The 2011 Minot's Souris River flood was of epic proportions. According to the US Army Corps of Engineers, the Souris River was estimated to flood at an interval between 200 and 500 years. The

Minot flood caught everyone off-guard when the Souris reached 1564 feet above sea level. The flood surpassed Minot's flood of 1969 when the Souris reached 1554.4 feet. It even surpassed the Minot flood of 1881 when the Souris reached 1558 feet.

The flood reached as far north as Saskatchewan and as far south as Minot. The flood started when Canada released water from two area dams to relieve the pressure on the local reservoirs. 11,000 Minot residents had to be evacuated, and farmlands were inundated with water. The Governor of North Dakota declared a state of emergency.

By the start of summer, the city of Minot was submerged. Over 4,000 homes were damaged or destroyed in Ward County alone. Costs neared one billion dollars.

Williston Flooding

Less substantial than the Minot flood was the impact of rainfall that flooded many Williston homes. Basements were submerged. Hundreds of thousands of dollars were lost. Work crews from outside the city were doing a brisk business removing carpet and replacing drywall if you could find them.

Inflationary costs soared yet again. Hundreds of millions in reconstruction projects related to Minot's flood added another inflationary punch. The Minot flood, combined with an aggressive oil market, made recovery efforts difficult. College employees had a hard time finding labor to address damaged homes.

In addition to flooding, Williston was coping with skyrocketing rents. One group of senior residents saw their rent increase from $700 per month to $2,000 per month. Oil companies bought entire apartment buildings, and tenants were evicted to make way for workers.

Williston State employees faced similar housing struggles. College employees, whose salaries were seriously lagging behind oil workers, talked about either finding a new job or leaving altogether. One employee took a job in the oil field because he was paid a $500 per month housing allowance. The employee already owned his home, so the allowance was just another form in which higher compensation was being offered. Williston was no longer affordable.

International Housing

A year earlier I felt I was making considerable progress with the on-campus housing; now I was quickly finding that I was on my way back to square one. The first of several formal requests came on behalf of instruction: "We would like to reserve a minimum of five trailers (and maybe up to eight trailers) for the fall 2011 school year for potential faculty positions." I purchased seven more trailers.

The opening of a new residence hall in the coming fall meant Dickson Hall would be vacant. The college did not have the money to tear down the building, nor was it able to have an empty building on campus. Dickson Hall was about to be turned into a transient super trailer.

A request came from the city asking the college to house J1 visa students. The request was motivated by an acute labor shortage. Unemployment in Williston was just under 1%. International J1 students, staying three months, had been housed in Dickson Hall previously during the summer. International students increased diversity on campus. They met a critical business and community need for workers – financially, too, as money collected would offset the bond payments of the new residence hall. This was a no-brainer. Welcome short-stay international student workers.

Dickson Hall was leased for three seasons beginning in June, December, and March. Sure, Dickson was in rough shape, but for a three-month live abroad experience where unskilled wages went from $15 to $25 per hour, the experience was a gold mine for international students. The project was a major success. The students described their co-op experience as their most valuable college experience. The college earned almost $250,000 per year. Local businesses were happy. Win, Win, Win. Almost.

Alone

The college and I were both in a bad place. Work was taking a heavy toll on staff morale. I wasn't sure if I had lost my family.

International student housing, a DMV, a trailer park, and a growing workforce-training program was a heavy burden for a small college. The strain was clearly visible on the staff. The finance office was short-staffed and in over their head. Student Affairs was not only running an expanding trailer park but was also taking care of the United Work and Travel contract (summer jobs program for international students). The faculty was stressed by a return to declining enrollment numbers as students left school for high paying, low skilled oil jobs.

Joyce left with the girls to spend the summer at her parents' home in New Jersey. I was alone on Father's Day, and I missed my daughter Julia's seventh birthday. I wasn't sure if Joyce would return. She had made friends in New Jersey over the summer. She felt reconnected. I busied myself with work. My head once again was elsewhere.

My family and the college were each quickly becoming a disaster. College morale needed to be addressed. A proposed bronze sculpture of Sitting Bull provided such an opportunity. We would have a party.

—

SITTING BULL[21]

"I surrender this rifle to you through my young son, whom I now desire to teach in this way that he has become a friend of the whites. I wish him to live as the whites do and be taught in their schools. I wish to be remembered as the last man of my tribe who gave up his rifle. This boy has now given it to you, and he wants to know how he is going to make a living."[22]

—Sitting Bull

The dedication of a Sitting Bull sculpture on campus took place the middle of summer. Besides a bronze at the city's library, the Sitting Bull sculpture would be the first piece of public art anyone could remember in years. Despite my good intentions, I ended up upsetting a good many people in the community and unwittingly ignited a multigenerational feud with the great grandson of Sitting Bull.

Once again, I incorrectly presumed that others would share my excitement about the college's first work of art. Many in the community asked why the college was putting an "Indian" at the front door of the campus. If Native Americans would not allow UND to use the Fighting Sioux nickname, why would the college commission a bronze of an "Indian."

Richard Stenberg took me to where Sitting Bull surrendered his rifle at Fort Buford in July of 1881. Sitting Bull, the famous Hunkpapa Sioux leader surrendered at Fort Buford just 25 miles from the college. The Friends of Fort Union had wanted to erect a heroic statue of Sitting Bull in front of the officers' quarters at Fort Buford to commemorate his return. The life-size statue was to be funded by the sale of smaller Sitting Bull statues, only twenty of which were made. Unfortunately, the statue was not well crafted, and the project fell apart and was ultimately abandoned.

One of the statues came into my possession. I decided to continue where the Friends of Fort Union left off. Instead of having the statue at Fort Buford, the statue would be erected at Williston State College. When Sitting Bull handed over his rifle to Major Brotherton, his message was one of education and hope, a message clearly needed in the community. The statue would be both a historic landmark and a lesson on the importance of education.

The college had to find the right artist. Michael Westergard, a prominent sculptor out of Plentywood, Montana was available. His artwork was in high demand and therefore somewhat expensive. But with the slowdown in the nation's economy, a window of opportunity opened.

Terry, Richard, and I sought permission from the Friends of Fort Union to pick up the project. When we found out Michael Westergard was available, we invited the artist to come out for a couple of consultations. Westergard looked at several different pictures of Sitting Bull provided by Professor Stenberg. Stenberg wanted Sitting Bull captured at a time when he was addressing his warriors, right after they turned in their horses at Fort Buford. Sitting Bull had admonished his warriors: "We're done. We've come home. No more."

Westergard worked on several proofs. A life-size cast of Sitting Bull was completed. In a rare instance of a Williston project finishing on time and within budget, the statue would be ready for the college to celebrate the 130th anniversary of Sitting Bull's return.

The dedication would take place in front of Williston State College. An invitation-only dinner would be held the evening before, and the artist would talk about the statue at both events. But who would talk about Sitting Bull?

The college contracted with Ernie Lapointe, the great-grandson of Sitting Bull. He had just completed a book on his great-grandfather and was doing the lecture circuit. Timing once again was impeccable.

The only job left was to line up entertainment. The last thing the college wanted to do was step on reservation politics. Who would entertain? How would the entertainment connect to the solemnity of the event?

Professor Stenberg and I spoke with a ranger at Fort Union, Loren Yellowbird. A Native American, he also worked as a Native American consultant in a string of Hollywood movies. His last picture was the Oscar-winning *The Revenant.* Loren recommended a Native American drummer, Earl Bullhead. A contract was signed with Mr. Bullhead. Everything was in place.

What neither Loren or we knew at the time was that Earl Bullhead was the great-grandson of one of the men who murdered Sitting Bull. The worse possible scenario came into play. The great grandson of the Sitting Bull and one of the great grandsons of the man who shot Sitting Bull would be together to introduce and celebrate the dedication of the Sitting Bull bronze.

Inviting Bullhead was the equivalent of asking the Oswald family to do the opening prayer for John F. Kennedy's memorial. Worse, even though the event happened nearly a hundred thirty years ago, a blood feud was still going on between the families.

I had read Ernie's book, and I knew about the blood feud. It was front and center in the narrative. The seriousness of the situation became evident when I received a call from Ernie.

Ernie was hot. He called me while I was on my way to Bismarck for a meeting and I immediately pulled over to the side of the road. Ernie hammered me for well over an hour. By the end of the conversation, I had pledged not to have Bullhead at the opening. I had apologized until my throat was dry. Ernie reluctantly decided that he would still attend.

So instead of breaking the contract with Mr. Bullhead, the college paid him not to perform. He threatened to come, but in the end, he either understood or was exasperated to the point where he gave up on us.

Even when Ernie arrived, he ruminated over his grandfather's death at the hands of Bullhead. His sense of past, his cultural pride went deep. He carried with him the traditions and respect of an incredibly proud people, and he literally wore their scars.

Ernie is also a Vietnam vet. Military service holds a source of tremendous pride for Native Americans. When attending Pow Wows, veterans and active military take pride of place at the front of the dance.

Ernie even participated in the Sun Dance ritual, not legal at the time of Ernie's initiation. Besides the Sun Dance ritual being the Lakota's most important ritual, it was dangerous. The initiated prays for the well-being of the community though a personal sacrifice. The ritual requires incredible personal suffering through the piercing of the skin. A length of bone, tethered to a pole is pegged through the skin of their chests. The dancers, having fasted for four days, slowly shuffle in a circle around the pole.

I shared my surprise at Ernie's participation in the Sun Dance ritual with Dakota Goodhouse, a program officer at the North Dakota Humanities Council who attended the dedication to give the final blessing. Dakota told me that he himself had undertaken a modified Sun Dance ritual. My head was spinning. There was so much I did not know or even could begin to understand.

I certainly had no context in which to understand Ernie's life. I struggled to understand both the Sun Dance ritual and the blood feud. But always, I listened to Ernie with grave respect. I truly felt I was in the presence of greatness.

Donn Skadeland

The North Dakota Highway Patrol has identified a 53-year-old pilot killed when a single-engine airplane lost power and crashed in a field near Williston. The patrol says a plane piloted by Donn Skadeland (SKAD'-lihnd) of Williston went down Monday night about 20 miles east of Williston. Skadeland was transported to a Williston hospital where he died of his injuries. A 55-year-old passenger, Gerald Gratz of Williston, also was taken to the hospital. His condition was not known.

—Bismarck Tribune, July 26, 2011

Just two weeks after the Sitting Bull dedication, Williston lost one of its own. Donn Skadeland, a hometown hero, was piloting his single-engine plane when he lost power and crashed into a field just east of Williston.

The only other person on the plane, Jerry Gratz, survived the crash. Jerry had recently sold his pharmacy, and when Don's business took off, Don hired his friend. Jerry was also a member of the college's foundation.

Don, a Williston native, was a gifted athlete and a celebrated member of Williston High School's 1975 State Championship Basketball team. Playing under Coach Terry Olson at the college and winning a state title, Don later became a major contributor to the college.

When Don played basketball (at that time in the old gym), all 650 seats were filled. Because of the size of the gym, the sound booming from the fans was like attending a Led Zeppelin concert. After his death, the college's gym was given a facelift and renamed the Don Skadeland Gymnasium.

Everyone knew Don. His death at 53 seemed to underscore that life in Williston had changed forever. The influx of people coming into Williston, the increase in truck traffic, the lack of basic services and a series of natural disasters were for many people a sign. The town was going through an identity crisis. Williston was no longer a small town, but what was to become of it?

Maybe, I thought, the college, the community, and my family were each going through its own modified Sun Dance ritual. Sometimes, it seemed the sacrifice was too much. Having stood next to Ernie, having mourned the death of Don, I was not about to bet against the resilience of this community. I was just beginning to understand my place in it.

—

DESPERATELY SEEKING ENROLLMENT

"An internal audit by the university system that was made public last week blamed Mr. McCallum for inflated enrollment numbers, which were posted not only in university documents but also in official reports to the U.S. Department of Education. Both the audit's findings and Mr. McCallum's failure to communicate with Mr. Goetz on the matter since last Wednesday were cited as grounds for his dismissal."

—The Chronicle of Higher Education, August 8, 2011[23]

Up until the boom, the number of high school graduates in North Dakota was dropping due to negative population growth. Colleges were under constant pressure to increase or at the very least maintain their enrollments. Many questionable enrollment practices materialized. In 2011, while the college was knee deep in the oil boom, an enrollment scandal not only rocked the university system but took a life.

The scandal involved Dickinson State University, the only public university in western North Dakota. Located in the southwest corner of the state, Dickinson borders Montana and South Dakota. Dickinson is a two-hour drive from Williston and just under a one-and-a-half-hour drive from Bismarck. Like all colleges in a state plagued by declining populations, Dickinson State was in a desperate scramble for enrollment.

To beef up their numbers, Dickinson had chosen to count students attending their Theodore Roosevelt Symposium and Walt Disney hospitality skills seminar. Two hundred and thirteen people enrolled in unqualified or what is traditionally called "non-credit" classes. The students received a credit grade of "A."

The attendees had no knowledge of the grade. The classes lacked syllabi, qualified instructors, and any form of assessment. The University knew the students did not qualify. And because the school counted the non-credit hours as credit, Dickinson saw an increase in their base funding from the state.

Not surprisingly, Dickinson State was caught. A state audit was conducted and matters were made worse when it was discovered that the scandal went deeper. Dickinson State University awarded hundreds of degrees to academically ineligible international students.

It is unclear whether the international students even had high school degrees. In an interview with the *Minot Daily News*, Chancellor Goetz stated, "the problem was limited almost exclusively to students from China who attended Dickinson State. An audit says in the last eight years, 400 of 410 foreign students who have gotten diplomas at Dickinson State didn't finish their degree work."

The enrollment pressure on 11 public universities in a state of just over 700,000 people is enormous. Only recently, primarily in Williston and Fargo, had there been an uptick in population. Before that, populations declined annually. As a result, the university system turned a blind eye to three highly questionable enrollment practices: false awards as in the case of Dickinson State; increasing certain groups of students, and dual credit. Each enrollment practice had the potential for significant impact on the credibility of the university system.

North Dakota colleges have historically offset low enrollments by increasing enrollment in specific student groups. Increasing the number of sports in a college is a good example. Generous athletic scholarships and waivers account for the extraordinary number of out-of-state athletes in each of North Dakota's eleven colleges. These athletes purchase meal plans, fill residence halls, and add state dollars to the college's budget.

On my arrival at Williston State, over half of the on-campus students were athletes in the college's sports program. The number of students in athletic programs was even higher in schools like Dakota College. In my second year as president of Williston State, Dakota College, a school of nearly 600 students, started a football team. Without the athletes on campus, I am not sure if Dakota College was viable.

Many North Dakota colleges actively grow enrollment through dual credit. Dual credit enrolls students in college courses while they are still in high school. The state pays the school district for the high school credit, and then the state pays a second time to the college when the high school class is identified as equivalent to a college-level course.

North Dakota State College of Science protects its dual credit enrollment like a feudal lord. Mayville State University, adjacent to two research universities, also turned significantly to dual credit. Located in a population of just over 2,000, Mayville State University taps into dual credit opportunities across the entire state to bolster its student numbers.

On my arrival, I questioned the university's practice of dual credit. At least a third of credits in schools like North Dakota State College of Science, Mayville State University, Lake Region State College and Williston State College are awarded via dual credit. The university system's attorney told me to back off.

The university system is not a happy system. There is no way it could be. Scarce resources coupled with a scant consumer base have led to petty antagonisms and parochialism. Just as pioneers created instant civilization, higher education created instant universities. No one wanted to shut down a college, so questionable enrollment practices continued, presenting an inflated number of students that attend classes on campus.

The State Board, on the other hand, chose to ignore the growth taking place in northwest North Dakota. A report[24] commissioned by the university system identified high growth in both Fargo and Williston. The report recommended expansion in the Bakken Region, specifically citing Williston State College. The expansion could have taken place by extending Williston State's education outreach to Watford City or Tioga. It could have taken place by expanding access to baccalaureate education at Williston State. It could have taken place by strengthening existing technical programs and offering new technical programs. But it didn't.

Colleges were not happy with the demographic shift taking place in the northwest. Colleges were funded based on student numbers, and Williston State was on track for significant growth meaning a possible redistribution of resources to this previously ignored institution. Most North Dakota colleges were in the eastern part of the state and the State Board, composed of members primarily from Bismarck eastward, chose to ignore the population growth in the northwest. While exasperating, the enrollment behavior and the tragedy that followed was not completely unexpected.

Bitter-Sweet Birthday

For my 50th birthday, the college held a surprise party for me in the library. Also on my 50th birthday, a dean from Dickinson State University committed suicide.

Douglas LaPlante, the dean of education, business, and applied sciences, had been reported missing at 9:27 a.m. after not showing at a meeting at the school. Officers responded to his home and found that he had left on foot, leaving behind his identification and cellphone.

A large caliber rifle was missing from his home. A passerby saw him walking toward Rocky Butte Park, where his body was found near the band shell. The police statement said the cause of death appeared to have been a self-inflicted gunshot wound. LaPlante was at the center of Dickinson's enrollment scandal.

While the university system struggled with the tragedy created by Dickinson State, Williston State was left alone. I was frustrated by the blind eye of the university system. I was even more frustrated by my community, which had come to accept the university system's blindness as a way of life.

The suicide cemented for me the idea that the university system would be of no assistance. Any consideration we had previously of expanding our offerings would now take a back seat to the college's survival. Safety, turnover, housing, and daycare issues were escalating quickly. The college needed help. It was time to roll out our big gun: Representative Skarphol.

Chapter 5
SPECIAL SESSION

"An accident is seen on the west side of Williston in early October. Police reported 131 vehicle accidents occurred in October this year, nearly double over October 2010."

—*Williston Herald, November 21, 2011*

UNSAFE

The vice president for student affairs stopped me in the hallway. One of the recruiters had recently attended a school meeting in Montana where parents expressed concerns that Williston was no longer safe, that the college itself was unsafe.

We were in the United States. Unsafe colleges? Unsafe colleges in North Dakota, where up until a year ago people didn't even lock their doors? Yet, everything around me validated the inescapable conclusion: Williston was indeed unsafe.

Hit and run accidents in Williston more than doubled from seventeen the prior October to thirty-nine. Vehicle damage from accidents went from $199,000 to $483,000. Williston Police attributed the across-the-board increases to the growth in population and traffic in the area. The most dangerous age group: ages 16–24.[25]

Incidents were happening daily. An individual was living in a white pickup truck parked outside of Nelson Hall. A Resident Assistant from Frontier Hall reported a man living in a truck parked outside of the diesel program. Another man was discovered sleeping on a couch outside of the bookstore. Staff and students were afraid to walk to and from their housing units.

Every morning, to relieve stress, I worked out at the college. I would finish my workout and then shower in the men's basketball locker room. As I was showering around 6:30 a.m. one morning, a young man entered the shower, which was usually empty except for myself. I initially thought he was a member of the basketball team and kidded him about being up so early for practice. He informed me he was not a member of the basketball team. I asked if he was a student. He was not.

Standing in the shower, I informed him that I was the president. His response: "I guess I should not be here." I told him no, he should not be here. I knew he didn't have housing and most probably spent the night in his car. I told him to finish his shower and leave.

From that day on, I made it a point to do one walk in the morning and one walk in the evening around campus. Each time I took a walk, I found someone loitering in a car outside one of the college's residence halls. I then would ask the person to leave campus. I added security to the head resident's job description.

The college did not have the means to afford adequate security. The new residence hall had only been open one month. Staff had already requested additional locks, cameras, key cards and daytime security. The cost for elevator security access controls had increased from $27,000 to $36,000 within two months of the initial bid. The college was being bankrupted in bits and pieces.

The stress was starting to show. People were afraid to walk to their cars at night. I had cameras and additional lighting but no one to install them. Even when the college could make things happen, we were at the mercy of the contractor's schedule. The soaring costs of labor had an impact at home as well. My in-laws came to visit, bringing to eight the number of people living in our home. It seems like the five toilets in our house should have been sufficient. However, the European-style toilets all gave out around the same time and nobody could get the replacement parts. We went several weeks with eight people sharing one bathroom. When we were finally able to get a contractor to fix the toilets, he had come from out of state, charged $60,000, and then never finished the job.

Turnover

"Some of (Williston State College English Professor) Stout's students have been trying to convince him to work for one of the oil companies – the last offer was to drive a truck 12 to 18 hours a day and get paid nearly $100,000 to start. Stout admits he's been tempted to make the switch: The lure of doubling his $56,000 a year salary is hard to resist." [26]

—*CNN*, November 1, 2011

With daycare increasingly unavailable, we started to lose employees. A company out of Chicago, called Rogy, worked with the city to identify the feasibility of setting up daycare on campus. The daycare need was dire. I offered Nelson Hall for their use at no charge. The college pledged an additional $25,000 in daycare assistance for our employee's children's use of the facility. Renovation costs, however, were prohibitive. Even with the offer of the building, promised subsidies from multiple businesses and potential funding from the city, Rogy could not create a sound business model for operating a daycare in Williston.

Most of the employees leaving the college identified economic factors as a reason for leaving, due to either salary or the increasing costs associated with housing and childcare. With low skilled jobs starting at $15 per hour, the college was priced out of the market.

In Williams County, where Williston is the seat, there were nine job openings for every resident looking for work. The top four wage earning cities were in western North Dakota, with Williston being the highest.[27]

Within a two-week span, both our vice president for administrative affairs and our vice president for student affairs resigned.

The vice president for administrative affairs (18 months on the job) accepted a much higher paying position as a vice president in one of the local banks. The finance office, again without a vice president, was in chaos.

Financial transactions were going through the roof. TrainND had increased training from 3,000 students to 10,000 students. The college's Small Business Development Center obtained more loans for small businesses in one month than the combined state SBDC's obtained in a year.

The university system could lend no assistance, and the college continued to fall further behind in its fiscal reporting. The biggest struggle though remained the shortage of housing. When people talked about a housing shortage in western North Dakota, they really meant NO housing. There was literally no place to sleep.

After one staff meeting, a veteran faculty member informed me that if he had one more rent increase, he would not be able to afford to live in his apartment. Another employee's rent went from $500 to $800 to $1200 in six months. Employees were effectively being priced out of housing.

"Busiest Town in America"

"The busiest town in America is not in New York, California or anywhere near Madison Avenue, Hollywood or Disney World, but out on the prairie near the geographic center of North America... Williston isn't just a city the recession forgot; it's [a] living, breathing example of just how bad the economy is everywhere else. It draws in people from as far as Florida and Texas, who leave everything behind in search of a well-paying job and whose tales of desperation shape this place."

—*Advertising Age*, October 31, 2011[28]

According to the 2010 Census, Williston (14,716) was North Dakota's ninth largest city. The population of Williston by 2011 was close to

22,000, almost double just two years after I arrived. Given the level of building and city annexations, it would be reasonable to expect another 18,000 people living within the city limits by 2016.

The oil patch cities were initially flexible, greeting all newcomers with open arms. But limits had been reached even for cities. The Watford City Council placed a moratorium on new man camps, and the Williams County Commission issued a six-month moratorium.

Somehow, amid the boom, the college managed to move forward. We opened the Western Star Career and Technology Center as well as the new Residence Hall. The first cohort of United Work and Travel Students arrived. The college and the foundation had initial discussions about a potential apartment building on campus. And after the devastation from the Tsunami, Kokusai Junior College sent its first cohort of students.

Williston and the college then did something remarkable. It took two elections, and a lot of campaigning, but the city passed a 1-cent sales tax to fund a $76 million recreation center on campus. The initial vote had missed its mark by 31 votes. When the Park District made the decision to partner with the college, placing the new recreation center on Williston State's Campus; Williston voters passed the measure by a two-to-one margin.

The college, regardless of its struggles, remained completely ignored by the State Board. The State Board neither requested nor was preparing a legislative request for Williston State, and Chancellor Goetz was under immense pressure because of the Dickinson State University scandal. The special session created an opening.

Because of the Minot flood, the Governor called a legislative special session. The problems facing Williston State were not part of the special session's agenda. Somehow, we had to figure out a way to put it there. Representative Skarphol would be key. My case was ready.

—

SPECIAL SESSION

Minot, the state's fourth-largest city, faces a severe housing shortage. It was bad enough when the booming oil industry brought thousands of workers to the area, and it's gotten worst after the worst flood in the city's history damaged some 4,000 homes along the Souris River this summer. But the challenge for developers is an equally big mismatch between supply and demand in the labor force. Rising demand for oil field workers has meant a shortage of construction workers, and consequently, rising wages.

—*Bismarck Tribune*, October 9, 2011[29]

Governor Dalrymple called for a Special Legislative Session, but it was not to deal with the oil boom. The session was called to discuss the damage done by the Minot flood. Since legislators and the State Board were still arguing over the Fighting Sioux nickname, it, too, was placed on the special session agenda.

It was widely believed that no bills would be introduced in the special session regardless of other crises happening in the state. The mayor, usually positive, was doubtful about Williston State making a special session request. What was the harm in asking? Over three years, the college moved from a low-cost rural environment to a high-cost environment like New York, but without the amenities.

The college was sinking, and the future looked bleak. We could not keep up with wages. Security on campus was close to nonexistent. Old buildings were in a state of disrepair and subject to unscrupulous costs. I requested and received approval from Chancellor Goetz to work with Representative Skarphol to seek two million dollars in one-time funding. Special session funding, although a long shot, was critical to Williston State.

Representative Skarphol introduced House Bill 1477 on behalf of the college. If funding were awarded, which looked highly unlikely, the college would have to continue to operate in a hyperinflation environment and hope the funding would become permanent in the next legislative session. Except for Representative Skarphol, our request was on no one's radar.

The State Board never formally approved Williston State's request to the legislature. They did attend, in full force, the legislature's discussion on the Fighting Sioux nickname. Their priorities were evident; they were absent when the college's bill was discussed in appropriations. I was the only person from the university system present.

Two Million Awarded

He (Nadolny) said the college has lost about one-quarter of its staff since spring as employees moved or, in some cases, were lured away by oil companies offering higher pay or better perks. At a special session earlier this month, all but two of the state's 141 legislators agreed to give WSC an additional $2 million of state funding, with practically no strings attached.

—*Grand Forks Herald*, November 21, 2011[30]

On the morning of November 10, Representative Skarphol sent the following message: "Your bill passed House 93-1. Bob" One hour later, he sent a second message: "The bill passed the Senate 46-1. Bob" We had received two million dollars in emergency funding.

Funding for the special session became available December 1, 2011, and was immediately used to address safety and employee retention/recruitment. The college mitigated asbestos, purchased a backup generator, hired daytime security, and added locks, cameras, and lighting to the residence hall. The college hired its first full-time counselor. And as the college had already lost three employees during the special session due to lack of childcare, $100,000 was set aside to address renovation and startup costs for a possible childcare center.

Unfortunately, Williston State was immediately hit with more unanticipated costs. The company the college contracted for evening security sent the following email: "I regret that I will have to raise our current hourly cost of $32 an hour to $40 per hour." The generator, initially priced at $300,000 would cost $450,000. Even with the funding, the college would have a hard time staying afloat. As I stated to the *Grand Forks Herald*:

> "I really believed that I could manage with the funding that was in place, but this growth came so fast and so sudden that it really caught us questioning, 'How do we react to something that is just so incredibly fast?'" Nadolny said. "I don't know if it's slowing down and I don't know where the peak is."[31]

Guardian Angel

One only had to read the national headlines to see that something both magnificent and terrible was taking place in the oil patch. Unfortunately, North Dakota was not accustomed to shifting its resources from the eastern part of the state to the western part. That included the State Board. Instead of being relieved that Williston State was bailed out by the legislature, the State Board made no reference to the award. We continued to operate in a vacuum.

I drove from Bismarck to the State Board meeting in Grand Forks when I received a call that my wife and two younger daughters had been involved in an auto accident. Joyce was taking her car to Minot in a blizzard when she hit black ice and lost control of the vehicle. The hospital was not sure if Joyce had suffered an injury to her liver, and the car was totaled so she and the two little ones were stranded two hours from home. I immediately left the meeting, drove five hours to pick up my wife and two daughters in Minot and drive another two hours back to Williston.

Joyce was devastated. She told me later that she thought she might die that day when without support of friends or family, she had to get on the road in a blizzard. Whereas people brought me food and gifts for many occasions, no one checked in on her after the accident and I was too busy with the college to offer much support. As I encountered victories, she suffered setbacks. I was too caught up in myself and my work to understand the gravity of my family situation.

On my return to Williston, I was treated like a hero. Special session funding was an enormous relief to the cash-strapped college. I was not a hero. I did, however, finally understand how North Dakota government works. The case for the college was great, well written and well delivered. What the college achieved came through the influence and power wielded by Representative Skarphol. With little to no State Board support, the college needed a guardian angel. Representative Bob Skarphol was that angel.

I was giddy with relief. Still, Williston had serious quality of life issues. There was no Starbucks or Barnes and Noble. There were few places for a person to hang out and feel like they were part of the community. The increase in traffic accidents mixed with skyrocketing inflation had people on edge. The city looked worse than when I arrived. The exception was the college. The college was making a difference.

At some point, the new recreation center, campus improvements, and the investment in infrastructure by the city and state would make a positive impact on Williston's quality of life. I could sense a tipping point. Prices had to come down eventually. When and where this would happen, I did not know.

I was too optimistic. Two million dollars can do that. No one could have ever have imagined that we were still only in the beginning of the boom.

Chapter 6
THE BOOM THAT ROARED[32]

When Nadolny became Williston State College president in 2009, he vowed to get rid of the seven mobile homes on campus. Instead he has about doubled the size of college's mobile home park to house faculty, staff and construction workers due to the severe housing shortage in the region. The housing issue, coupled with so many other job opportunities in the area, contributed to a 40 percent staff turnover rate at the college last year.[33]

—"Faces of the Boom," by Amy Dalrymple,
Fargo Forum, February 26, 2012

CSI WILLISTON

A sex offender on campus, rampant staff turnover, soaring crime and widespread transiency only added to the trauma for Williston as a mass influx of out of state workers sought refuge from a nationally recessed economy. The boom was now in its third year, and the campus was under siege. The college was struggling to protect a vulnerable, young, and primarily female student and staff population. Two million in emergency funding was not enough to assist a college coping with a tsunami of its own.

Family Flight

Each year, my family spent time in New Jersey. Once again, I would not be joining them due to the many challenges that needed my attention on campus. If I had attended, I would like to think things would have turned out differently.

For this vacation, the family had rented a house in upstate New Jersey. During my family's stay, Joyce's mom fell down a flight of stairs and broke her leg. She shattered bones throughout the left side of her body and was in the hospital for five weeks. For months, she was confined to a wheel chair. My mother-in-law was the primary caregiver for my father-in-law. Now they both needed care.

Joyce, already feeling abandoned in Williston, jumped at the chance to stay in New Jersey and help her parents. She transferred the girls from their schools in Williston to schools in New Jersey. I was alone.

While my children attended school in New Jersey, the Williston School District was dealing with a flood of new students. Superintendent Viola LaFountaine was worried: "We're on the cliff; we're on the edge. We are in such financial straits that we don't have the funding to even lease or purchase modulars right now."[34]

The school district would eventually purchase 34 FEMA trailers to address record enrollment numbers. The FEMA Trailers, temporary manufactured housing units the government used to deal with the Minot flood, were available for purchase. Minot didn't need the trailers because of massive state and federal funding. Minot was in the process of building and renovating the flood-damaged schools, so the Williston school district scooped the discarded FEMA trailers up.

The Williston School District had a plan for a new school. It just didn't have the money. When the superintendent announced the purchase of the trailers, they sounded more permanent than temporary. The permanent nature of the trailers was just another example of the "Williston experience." The 34 FEMA trailers are still used as classrooms today.

If Julia and Emma returned to school in the fall, and that was a big "if," they would be entered into a lottery for a school two blocks down the street from our home. If they were not selected, they would have to attend school in one of the school district's recently acquired FEMA trailers.

If my family did return, what would I be bringing them back to? A year earlier, the school district had 19 students classified as homeless. In 2012, that number jumped to 170. The idea of FEMA trailers as classrooms was reminiscent of the Adult Education Trailer in the Campus' mobile home park. One of the teachers scheduled to teach in a FEMA trailer told me the trailers were actually "very nice." I heard similar comments from my faculty when I first arrived at the college. Faye said that her closet, converted into an office and occasionally resulted in headaches, was nice. North Dakotans are tough, but they would need to be a lot tougher for what still lay ahead. Like all booms, this one packed a punch. Unlike other booms, this one continued to hit.

Sherry Arnold

The abduction and death of Sherry Arnold was the boom's first real tragedy. Sherry was born and raised on a ranch 44 miles from Williston in Sidney, Montana. In grade school, she had the nickname "bright eyes."

Sherry graduated valedictorian of her class and attended the University of North Dakota-Williston, where she played on the college's volleyball team and graduated with an associate's degree. She earned her bachelor's degree in math from Dickinson State University. Sherry taught in Tioga, Minot, and for 18 years in Sidney, Montana. Married and the mother of two children, she was well liked and well respected both in northwest North Dakota and northeast Montana.

An avid runner, Sherry was also known for her determination. For six years, she struggled with a rare cancer. As with most things Sherry tackled, she overcame it.

On January 10, Sherry was reported missing, having never returned from a pre-dawn run. About the same time, Lester Van Waters Jr., 48, and Michael Keith Spell, 22, from Parachute, Colorado were looking for work in the oil fields.

Spell had a one-year-old son and moved to Williston when he heard about jobs paying up to $2000 per week. According to his father, Spell had less education than a kindergartner. At trial, Spell testified he was illiterate. Waters, on the other hand, had a lengthy criminal background and had served time in the state prison.

According to Spell, Sherry said "Hi" as Spell and Waters passed her on the path. As she passed, Spell turned around and hit her on the back of the head knocking her down. Spell choked Sherry and held her face under water until she was dead.

Law enforcement, family, friends, and the community spent two months searching for Sherry. Her body was finally found on Highway 1804, east of Williston. The body was laying in a fetal position in a shallow grave allegedly dug by Waters. Her grave rested alongside a shelterbelt, a line of trees used by farmers as a shield from the wind.

The tragic and brutal death of a much-loved community member was a wake-up call. The oil boom brought tremendous opportunity, but it also brought enormous tragedy. North Dakota ranked as the most outgoing state, the most livable state and one of the top ten states for child well-being. That was no longer true, at least for western North Dakota.

Just the summer prior, Don Skadeland died in an airplane accident. His death had been indirectly chalked up to the oil boom as he was assessing the opportunities available to his business because of the boom. Sherry's death was different. Sherry's death was a direct outcome of the oil boom. Those men, Waters and Spell, would never have been in the area otherwise.

At the 2011 January in-service, I talked about Sherry Arnold. Sherry was family, and although no one believed she would be found alive, the confirmation of her death came as a painful blow. As I told

Sherry's story, some of the staff began to cry. It took three years for the reality to sink in: the boom was here to stay. It was then that I laid out new ground rules for the college.

Campus Wake Up Call

> The Williams County Sheriff's Office in Williston reports that there are as many DWIs issued at 10 a.m. as are issued at midnight. Jail bookings have increased 150 percent, and bonds as large as $10,000 are routinely paid in cash. (One person paid a $65,000 bond by pulling the cash out of a Walmart shopping bag.) Law enforcement can no longer do anything but answer calls, make arrests and investigate crimes... The North Dakota Sheriffs & Deputies Association states that in Williston and Williams County civil process servings went from fewer than 2,000 per year to more than 4,000 last year.[35]
>
> —Indian Country Media Network, March 15, 2012

All staff members were now required to lock their offices at night. My guidance went unheeded the last time I made the request. This time it was a demand.

People were told to buddy up when walking on campus. No one walked alone. This was especially true at night. Everyone needed to make sure they had an escort to their vehicle.

The staff was required to turn off their cars when parking on campus. This may seem odd unless one understands North Dakota's climate. In a safe community with temperatures well below zero, it was common practice to leave one's car running when shopping or dropping in and out of a location. The new directives were grudgingly heeded.

The first couple of weeks of the spring semester gave credence to the new guidelines. During the week of in-service, tragedy struck. An international student with the United Work and Travel Program died in a car accident. Arthur, a student from Brazil, was a passenger in a car with three others. He was headed back to Williston after a few days of snowboarding in South Dakota. The driver of the car lost control on the icy road. The car flipped over and slid under a fast moving 18-wheeler. Arthur was killed instantly. Two other international students from Brazil and another local young man were also in the car. One was in stable condition and was released. Another student was in critical condition and was released later. The students were employed at Williston's McDonalds. Most of the international students were working two if not three jobs.

When classes began, a larger-than-usual number of students did not return. I had met four students that worked full-time jobs at Halliburton over the break. The money was too good. Three of the four students did not return for the spring semester.

A week after in-service, a drunk driver pulled into the college's parking lot, fell asleep at the wheel and crashed into Stevens Hall, the college's main academic building. Fortunately, no one was injured, but the rash of random accidents had everyone alarmed.

More and more emails were coming from parents of prospective students concerned about what they were reading in their local newspaper. One parent emailed me directly: "Hi, my daughter is considering going to school at WSC, and my main concern is the safety of the campus and surrounding area. We are from Billings and our newspaper, of course, reports all the negative stories. Is there any information you could give me concerning the safety of the students who attend and live on campus?"

Students continued to complain about inadequate lighting at the back of residence hall. I pleaded with the contractor. There was nothing I could say or do to expedite the repairs. The college was low on the priority list.

As security concerns heightened, Blackhawk Security recommended Whitey, the daytime security officer, carry mace and a Taser. Others wanted Whitey to carry a gun. Whitey's job was not to intervene; it was to call 911. But I relented and sent him to a safety seminar so he could carry mace to protect himself.

Walking to the college one morning, I saw a line that went outside the college door. I became a little nervous and asked the first person I met what was going on. The individual told me the people were in line to sign up for a concealed weapons course. The people in line were not the newcomers that had recently moved to Williston to find work in the oil fields. They were long-time community members registering for the course that would allow them to legally protect themselves with concealed weapons.

Not one month later, I issued another mandate requiring every employee and every non-student in college housing to go through an FBI background check. Running background checks was an incredibly burdensome task, both for the one-person human resource officer and the companies that had to wait until their employees were vetted by the college.

The rule was instituted the day after I read an alarming story in the city's Sunday newspaper. The *Williston Herald* ran an article on sex offenders that had moved into the community. Over the past sixteen months, the number of registered sex offenders doubled from forty-three in 2010 to eighty-six in 2011. The increase in sex offenders, however, was not what startled me.

The paper included a list of the sex offenders and their addresses. To my surprise – and I was starting to think I could no longer be surprised – one of the sex offenders was a construction worker for the new science wing. He was living in one of the college's mobiles.[36]

The college had several construction companies in college housing. Most were from out of town, and the cost of construction was significantly reduced if housing was part of the contract. Now I faced another dilemma. Was I able to have the person removed from the trailer?

I spoke to the foreman. He promised to have the man relocated to another one of their sites across town. From that day on, all full-time employees and individuals living in the mobile units were required to be fingerprinted so they could be run through the FBI's database.

—

BOOM TOWN

"**1 a:** a rough or uncouth person **b:** rowdy, tough; **2:** a worker of an oil-well-drilling crew other than the driller."

—*Merriam-Webster* definition of "Roughneck"

Transportation in and out of Williston was a nightmare. The Williston train depot was now the busiest stop between Seattle and Chicago. With the amount of oil being transported via rail, constant delays became the norm. A friend of Joyce's visiting from Seattle sat 17 hours on the train just 20 minutes outside of Williston because of a freight train derailment. With massive freight traffic, there was no predicting when passenger trains would arrive or leave. Timetables no longer mattered.

Travel by air was no better. Great Lakes Airlines, referred to by locals as Great Mistakes, was the sole providee. It would be another year before Delta and United entered the market. But until then, Williston was stuck with prop plane service to and from Denver. Councilman Bekkedahl, now Senator Bekkedahl, would drive the two-plus hours to Minot just to avoid Great Lakes.

The majority of Great Lakes passengers were "roughnecks." The roughnecks flew into town to work the oil fields two weeks on, two weeks off. The language on the plane was so vulgar it would make a sailor blush. Williston was crudely mocked and put down. The few families on the plane were rural country folk, and what they heard only strengthened the antagonism between the locals and outsiders looking to make a quick buck.

Driving was the most dangerous mode of transportation by far with the tremendous increase in large truck traffic. Everyone had a near death truck story to tell. Truck traffic also created a heavy concentration of dust, covering everything. The dust exacerbated respiratory illness and damaged the surrounding property and crops.

To address the problem, the state was building a bypass to divert trucks from driving through downtown Williston. A major project, the bypass would take almost two years to complete, which added even more frustration as people began to experience abnormally long traffic jams.

Travel between Williston and the surrounding communities of Tioga and Watford City had become dangerous. In the past, the distance between the cities allowed students to drive back and forth to the college. Given road construction and the large number of sixteen wheelers on the road, the college stopped recruiting in these cities unless the students were going to live on campus. I had two daughters in high school. If I would not allow them on the roads, I would certainly not invite others, no matter how hungry the state was for enrollment.

Limited access to the college resulted in a lot more students living on campus. The residence halls had a long waitlist. In most college towns, if a college's residence hall was full, students rented an apartment in town, but rents in Williston were beyond the reach of students.

A compromise was struck. The college purchased additional beds to meet the demand created by the waitlists. A third bed was placed in the two-person bedrooms. Students received a discount on housing, and the college accommodated more students.

Housing

"The most expensive place to rent new housing in the US isn't Miami, LA or even New York. Thanks to the fracking boom, it's Williston, North Dakota, where Walmart pays $20/hour and new arrivals sleep in shipping containers. How does a city cope with a modern-day gold rush?"[37]

2012 was the year Williston went from being a quiet, country town to something that resembled the wildness one hears about during the

California Gold Rush. Even Walmart had become a "Truck Camp." The city was a mess.

As people were getting squeezed on rents, the community became increasingly volatile. Some people desperate to keep their jobs made the decision to enroll in college just to take advantage of the college's housing. The residence hall now had several men in their forties and fifties living there. Conflicts emerged because of the older men living with a primarily young, female population, so the college instituted an age requirement. The residence hall would only accept students between ages 18 and 24.

Employees were struggling with housing even with the bonuses provided through the state's emergency session dollars. The vice president of administrative affairs saw his rent increase by over one thousand dollars per month in less than a year. Although bonuses were given to keep employees, employees started to question whether the one-time dollars would continue to be available in the next biennium.

Williston State was not immune to the desperation of the homeless either. Campers still pulled up to the residence halls to use external outlets. Trailer parks were no longer affordable and workers needed to stay warm.

The college approved a contractor's request to add three additional trailers on campus to support the additional workers necessary for the new recreation center, with the requirement that the contractor build a privacy fence around the trailer. Background checks were required for all workers. To the frustration of contractors, a growing number of workers were denied residency on campus due to felony convictions.

As the Science wing was nearing completion, the college's security officer found one of the construction workers living in the science wing. The college could afford neither the cost nor yet another delay in the completion of the science wing. The college turned a blind eye.

The security officer found men living in trees in the back of campus. When the security officer asked them to leave, they returned a day later. This time, he called the police. The police came, and the men moved. The men returned three days later. Exasperated and without any real options, I had campus services cut the trees down.

Without available hotel rooms in the city, my house often served as sleeping quarters for those doing business with the college. I brought a former dean from my previous college in Washington to help deal with the collapse of our technical programs. He lived in my basement for three months. When members of our sister college came to visit, they were housed at our home. When new faculty arrived, they temporarily lived at our house. Even people from the university office stayed in our home as hotel prices became either to high or unavailable. Joyce was a trooper, but she had no say or choice in those decisions and, in effect, I was subordinating home life again for the needs of the college.

There was no end in sight for northwest North Dakota's economic hyper growth, and as had become the pattern, Terry stepped in to make yet another difference. Terry made affordable housing a top priority. Housing development was not in Terry's job description. But he extended himself, getting buy-in from key constituency groups like the Governor's Office.

Terry proposed that the college foundation build an apartment building on campus. The building would take a year to construct, but it would provide affordable housing for college employees, law enforcement, Williston School District employees and state workers. Terry and I hoped that over time, the apartments would convert into student housing. The four-story apartment had a price tag of $10 million and would take a year to build, but it would become an important tool in the college's efforts to recruit and retain employees.

Wage Inflation

"Back then, city officials had a running joke about how easy it was to land work. You needed only a pulse," said Cindy Sanford, who manages the government-run jobs services office in town. "We laughingly would say, 'Breathe on a mirror... OK, try again,'" she recalled. Even the waitresses bragged about earning more than $700 per day."[38]

Between June 2009 and June 2011, the college's service area added 14,185 employees.[39] One-third of college employees would leave in 2012 for better opportunities provided in the oil patch. If the college received two to three applications for a position, people got excited. More frequently the college received zero to one application for every job opening, and rarely was an applicant qualified.

The college could not keep pace with salaries as there seemed to be no ceiling on employee wages. The lowest-paid custodian in 2009 was making $18,000 per year; now custodians were making a minimum of $30,000 per year. The college still could not hire a custodian to save its life.

Holding on to technical faculty was impossible. The pay for diesel technicians was approaching the obscene. The College lost both diesel instructors to oil companies. Replacement instructors had neither the experience nor the knowledge base. Parents of diesel students were outraged and started making complaints to the chancellor's office.

The college began to use emergency dollars to hire temporary employees from a job placement service. Most of these workers had just arrived in town, and as expected, some did not even have housing. The high-priced temporary employees had to be constantly managed, which created an additional workload and added to an already stressful employment situation at the college. The college eventually stopped using the service.

Employers throughout the city found themselves on a mad hunt for employees. I started to go to church a little earlier and stay a little later in the hopes of striking up a conversation with someone looking for a new job. I even attended a church of a different denomination to expand my recruitment efforts.

Even TrainND, the college's non-credit arm, was experiencing turnover. A noncredit program, TrainND was in the enviable position of being able to pay wages closer to the market rate, some jobs paying six figures. Since college employees knew about the high wages, they started moving into the open TrainND positions. The college's chief information officer resigned to accept a position as a TrainND trainer. His new salary was almost 50% higher.

Employers were calling me, increasingly frustrated that they could not find enough student workers to fill open positions. Students were constantly offered jobs with high pay and incredibly flexible hours, some even working two jobs. I had to stop taking staff to Chamber of Commerce events and Rotary luncheons for fear that other members would recruit them. College staff was young, most of my senior administrators in their mid- to late- twenties with little experience. They were still highly sought after by the quickly expanding businesses in town.

With the loss of yet another vice president of business affairs, the business office was disorganized (if not undone). For six weeks, the college had not received one application for the open VP position. We were in no position to match industry wages to recruit, much keep a VP for finance. I met with the chancellor and the vice chancellor for finance to devise a solution.

With the permission of both the chancellor and the vice chancellor for finance, the college's budget director, James, was promoted to vice president for business affairs. A week later, I received an email from the chancellor's assistant: "Morning! James was in our office and has been fully indoctrinated by the front office. He seems nice but when did you start hiring fourteen-year-olds?"

The turnover began to take a more personal toll. Hunter Berg, the college's athletic director and a local hero, confronted with his family leaving for Bismarck, resigned. It was the first time I cried in public. To make matters worse, Terry was crying with me. Berg's departure was a huge loss, but we couldn't begrudge him for making the decision to leave. Williston was no longer an easy or a safe place to raise a family.

DMV Turnover

The DMV did not turn out to be the recruiting mecca the college had hoped. With starting salaries at $40,000 per year, a string of customer incidents, and higher turnover than the college, Williston State was having serious thoughts about its ability to maintain the DMV.

One employee recently hired was subpoenaed to appear in court in Montana. She left saying she would be gone only a few days. She called back saying the trial took longer than expected. Then her car broke down in Wolf Point, Montana. The college waited and waited and waited. She never returned. She had accepted another position in Williston.

The college approved hiring two additional employees in anticipation of more turnover. The first person hired informed the human resource office she was already looking for other opportunities. She found that "other opportunity" the week she started. The second employee came to work in large, brown, fluffy slippers. One of the college's vice presidents told her to go home and change her shoes. She went home, picked up the phone and left a voicemail saying she would not be returning.

Things got so bad that an applicant walked into the HR Director's Office and was immediately offered the job. The man accepted. When asked to fill out the background check so he could get his keys, he filled in his name on the form and paused. He needed to get his glasses from his car. The HR Director never saw him again.

Day after day, long DMV lines formed out the door into the hallway. But between the college and the foundation, real doubt began to form on whether Williston State could follow through on the service. Something needed to be done. The college did not want to lose face with the Department of Transportation. The college had earned considerable goodwill from local legislators and the governor's office by carrying the burden of the DMV. And the community needed a functioning DMV. But the college had to stop the bleeding coming from the DMV.

Exhausted

The college needed to take a step back. Faculty and staff were overworked. I had to act, so I started by ending the United Work and Travel contract.

It was good having international students on campus, and the money was critical to the residence hall bond payment. But both the student affairs office and the finance office were completely overwhelmed. I sent an email to United Work and Travel that the college had made the decision to terminate the contract at the end of the year.

A week later, the city of Williston sent a letter officially requesting the extension of the United Work and Travel contract. The letter cited employee shortages and praised the college and our efforts to lighten its load. I talked to the finance staff and the student affairs staff. Despite their workload, they supported a contract extension. I extended the contract. Privately, I was grateful for the excuse to do so. I enjoyed having the international students on campus. Sure, the revenue from the contract was great, but it was even more rewarding knowing the difference these young workers were making in the community.

The community continued to reach out to the college. The Governor created the position of Energy Impact Coordinator, affectionately known as the Oil Czar. The Governor called and asked if the Energy Impact Coordinator could be housed at Williston State. I was not about to say no, and despite space issues, we found a space for the impact coordinator in the new technical building. So much for taking a step back.

Traumatized College

It was only when staff attended a mandatory accreditation training held in Chicago that they began to openly discuss the various traumas they were experiencing. Dr. Tim Gallimore, Vice President for the Higher Learning Commission (HLC), listened to several of the staff share stories of near death truck incidents, rising rents, and lack of childcare. Dr. Gallimore pulled me aside. He had several thoughts on the matter.

Dr. Gallimore was a former spokesperson for the prosecutor of the International Criminal Tribunal for Rwanda (ICTR). His personal experience involved losing his three brothers and two sisters during the killings that took place in Rwanda. Dr. Gallimore was well aware of the stress placed on communities as a result of violence, poor infrastructure, and rapid change.

He told me it was easier for him to deal with mass murders in Rwanda than the daily travel on the one road to Rwanda's capital city. The roads were crowded, filled with trucks and very dangerous. His comments resonated with me instantly. It sounded like Williston.

Two months later, Dr. Gallimore flew up to Williston to speak at the college's fall in-service. At the beginning of his presentation, he asked staff to raise their hands if they thought life was getting worse in Williston. Three-quarters of employees raised their hands.

Dr. Gallimore told staff they needed to identify ways to turn adversity into opportunity. He reminded us that the Williston community was fragile and numerous events were destabilizing the college. He heard about a recently discovered meth lab in Nelson Residence Hall, how upset some staff members had become by the escalating confrontations occurring at the DMV, and empathized with the problems facing an inexperienced staff that continued to operate under tremendous fiscal pressure with little direction or assistance from the university system.

He then said something very profound that tapped into the autonomous nature of the "go it alone" North Dakotans. The college must remember that the community was the college's resource. Communities help us to remain healthy. Everything we needed was in the community. We just needed to take back control.

The college's overwhelming experience was primarily rooted in a loss of control, the destruction of the community, itinerancy, and a lack of connection. He challenged us to open up. Dr. Gallimore exhorted staff to take back control. It was okay to feel isolated. But the college needed to disclose the vulnerabilities they faced. It was the first step in the healing process.

I could sense the relief in the room. Dr. Gallimore validated what the college was experiencing. The trauma the community was facing was real. Dr. Gallimore could not have come at a more critical time.

Looking Forward

Each month the mayor invited four to five community leaders to join him for lunch. Matt Grimshaw, the CEO of the hospital and I had received standing invitations. In the chaos of the boom, the mayor of Williston, Ward Koeser, offered a message of hope and encouragement. The mayor talked about a turning point. He believed the city would turn the corner in three years, and he was correct.

In a little over a year, people would not just be talking about oil in Williston; they would be talking about the $76 million indoor recreation center. And over the course of the construction of the Recreation Center, Ward promised the opening of multiple retail stores and restaurants.

Ward was a man of his word. Over the next three years, the quality of life in Williston would improve. Sewer relief, a truck stop, retail and restaurant development, recreation center, housing assistance, and an expanded college and hospital would turn the community around. Williston was becoming a much younger and much more diverse city.

People from as far east as Sidney, Montana and as far north as Weyburn, Canada, would travel to Williston not just for jobs but recreation and shopping. With Matt Grimshaw's leadership, people would see significant improvements in the quality of health care. And with Deanette Piesik's leadership, the CEO of TrainND, the college would continue to expand workforce training and higher education access. For the first time, people were no longer talking about making a quick buck, they were talking about making a home. We now believed it would only take a few more years for the city to build itself into something more than a town known for its man camps and strip clubs. The real question was how to make it through the next several years.

Over the time Joyce and the family were away in New Jersey, Williston moved from an obscure North Dakota town to the topic of stories in major newspapers both domestic and foreign. And to my complete surprise, Joyce returned home with the girls. The kids would start school in the fall.

My family was back, and the college was limping but operational. But I failed to see that Williston was in the eye of a hurricane. Progress might have been made, but the reality was that we were only living in a brief respite from the storm.

Chapter 7
COMPROMISED

"I want to do the right things, and I'm going to do it as consultatively as possible and as humanely as possible, but change is not something that is comfortable to a lot of people," he said. "In order to improve a system, in order to move forward, there has to be some changes made." Robert Vallie, the Board of Higher Education's student member, opposed the hiring, saying he feared Shirvani would be viewed as "a polarizing figure" [40]

CHAMPION

Chancellor Goetz was retiring. Future chancellors would be hired from out of state. Each thought they knew better and each would make significant mistakes as university system neglect would turn to outright interference.

Chancellor Goetz spent his last couple of months championing the college. He had taken the presidents to task on their refusal to allow Williston State to expand its educational offerings. In opposition to legal counsel, he allowed the college to assume the risk of the United Work and Travel contract. He even chastised the system's attorney for not understanding what was taking place in western North Dakota. Unfortunately, no one was listening. Now, he was leaving.

At Chancellor Goetz's last board meeting, he recommended a 3% salary increase for the university system's presidents... with one exception. The chancellor recommended a 6% increase for the president of Williston State. The recommendation passed with a unanimous vote.

I felt honored by the chancellor's recognition. I was also very conscious of the stares of my fellow presidents. As with the special session, Williston State was once again receiving special treatment. The perceived "favoritism" did not go over well with my colleagues. As a volunteer president, I was supposed to have known that the extra work "came with the territory."

Williston State lost the one champion it had in the system with the retirement of Chancellor Goetz, and it fell on me to make a strong case for the college. As the state's commerce department had little information on the impact of the oil boom, I conducted my own. With a transition occurring in the university system, I was left alone to make a case for the college's very survival. If the legislature did not continue the one-time funding provided in the special session, the college would undoubtedly break down under the weight of the relentless inflationary pressures.

Making the Case

"Ten years ago Williston, North Dakota was a quiet agricultural town with a population around 12,000. Today, because of oil prices and drilling advancements, Williston is home to America's biggest oil boom and its residents number over 30,000. Home prices are soaring, unemployment is close to zero and people from around the country are flocking here for jobs where the starting pay can easily exceed $100,000."[41]

—*Business Insider*, March 7, 2012

Ninety percent of the current drilling activity occurred within a 70-mile radius, making Williston the location of choice for oil and gas businesses looking to set up shop in North Dakota. The city of Williston was growing up.

Western North Dakota's growth and resulting issues were very like those experienced by the United States in the 19th century. At the end of the 19th century, 60.4% of the country's population was rural. By 2000, that number dropped to 39.6%. By 2012, that number was 15%. North Dakota and the country's rural population were now the minority.

Cities like Williston, Tioga, and Watford City had never made the jump from rural town to city. Because of the oil boom, the jump had become a leap. People were flocking into town from out of state. But another migration was taking place, too. North Dakotans were migrating from rural areas in North Dakota to the oil patch cities. The internal migration patterns were like the internal migration patterns of 20th century America. Western North Dakota was urbanizing.

I had personally seen this happen over the last ten years in cities like Ho Chi Minh and Shanghai. Each of these cities, like Bismarck with its growing state government and Williston with its growing oil economy, had become the hub of incredible economic opportunity and prosperity.

As the major cities of Bismarck, Grand Forks, Minot, Dickinson, Williston, and Fargo grew in population, the counties surrounding them declined. The press reported on the many people that traveled from out of state to North Dakota for the jobs created by the state's new wealth. Not reported on were the people moving from the rural counties surrounding these cities for the same opportunities. The rural population of North Dakota was in decline. And traditional rural towns, like Williston, were turning into cities.

Historically, Grand Forks and Fargo were the well-established cities in the east. Bismarck and Minot were the well-established cities in the center. Dickinson was the well-established city in the southwest. The oil boom created five additional "cities," all in the Northwest: Williston, New Town, Stanley, Tioga, and Watford City.

These new northwestern cities struggled from growing pains as they tried to maintain their rural character amidst the growth. The struggle was clearest in Williston's mayoral election. When Ward

Koeser stepped down after twenty years, the choice for a new mayor was between a long-time community member and an out of state business entrepreneur. The election became a decision between the rural integrity of Williston and the inevitability of urban growth. It was a heated race, but the long-time community member won.

The state's rural nature was also challenged in North Dakota's most recent gubernatorial election. Wayne Stenehjem ran against Doug Burgum. Stenehjem, the State's Attorney General, represented the "old guard" and was heavily endorsed by the North Dakota Republican Party. Burgum, also a Republican but with no formal political experience was an entrepreneur and philanthropist. This time, North Dakota voted for change and elected Burgum governor.

Williston was now the epicenter for new business and job growth. As the mayor predicted, restaurants and shops were opening. A new airport was planned. Roads were being repaired and expanded. Williston's economic impact could be felt as far east as Minneapolis and as far west as Miles City, Montana. The incredible regional impact of the oil boom was affecting the nation.

When I completed my research on the impact of the oil boom, I showed the numbers related to the demographic shifts to Larry Skogen, the president of Bismarck State College. He replied: "What this data also demonstrates is that the "business-as-usual" model is simply not going to address industry needs. If we as a system are not proactive and innovative, someone else will be. When that happens— because it will happen—we'll have only ourselves to blame, methinks." As I wrapped up my research, I felt prepared to meet with the incoming legislators.

Legislators Tour Oil Patch

Legislators were eager to discover first-hand what was taking place in the oil fields. Everyone wanted to know about the oil phenomenon. The number of legislative committees meeting in Williston was astonishing. Just over three-quarters of the North Dakota's legislators would visit the college and tour the northwest region that summer.

The visits were a success. The legislators felt like they had become experts on the Bakken. They enjoyed their stay in the residence hall (as, again, Williston hotels were no longer offering state rates). One could even say they bonded. I took a walk through the residence hall to see how the legislators were doing. One senator in a playfully hushed voice said: "Quick, put the alcohol away, the president is coming."

When I later requested a change in the reauthorization of TrainND's building project—initially thought to be $3.9 million and with a new price tag of $6.7 million—at the joint budget section meeting in Bismarck, something incredible happened: I was spared the traditional president's thrashing.

But no amount of research, no amount of reason, could protect the college from what was developing from within the university system: the arrival of a new chancellor. With this change, the college's story would be further lost in a sea of university system conflict and intrigue. The special funding awarded to Williston State during the special session would not even be integrated into the university system's request to the legislature. The college, once again, would be left on its own. And any attempts to educate the new chancellor on the challenges facing the college would fall on deaf ears.

—

REIGN OF TERROR

The State Board voted 5-3 to hire Dr. Hamid Shirvani, President of California State University Stanislaus. Shirvani, an architect by training, came with impeccable academic credentials. He received his masters from Harvard and his doctorate from Princeton. A devout Roman Catholic, Shirvani and his family left his native country of Iran to escape religious persecution.

Shirvani was leaving California amidst some controversy having recently received a vote of no confidence from faculty. Even with the controversy, Shirvani was given a salary of $340,000, higher than the posted salary range. Grant Shaft, Board President, made sure that Shirvani's pay was higher than the system's highest paid president, University of North Dakota's president Dr. Robert Kelly.

The message was clear. Shirvani would take charge of the presidents. He would start by addressing two long-term concerns. The first was the long-running controversy about the University of North Dakota's Fighting Sioux nickname—still not resolved. The second concern was the aftermath of the Dickinson State University diploma mill scandal.

Williston State College and the oil boom were not on the list of university system's concerns. For Williston State, the boom was a challenge and a struggle. For the other ten colleges, the boom was an opportunity wrapped in a rising state budget and a new source of students from the growing West.

Shirvani started his first day saying exactly what people wanted to hear: "People say California. I'm not coming from San Francisco. I am not a Beverly Hills person," he said. "Most of my board members never (wear) ties... and they drive pickup trucks, and in fact, I will be driving a truck too."

Shirvani's first visit to Williston State coincided with the State Board meeting being held in the city. Because of steep hotel prices, the new chancellor and his wife, Fatemah, stayed at my home. The chancellor did not pull up in a pickup truck; he owned a Ferrari.

When Shirvani met with the college's executive cabinet, I gave a brief rundown of the activities at the college. The college's contract training numbers were skyrocketing; WSC was partnering with the foundation to build a 72-unit apartment complex on campus to address the housing demands of college and state employees. The college was partnering with the Parks District to further improve the quality of life through a $76 million recreation center on campus. Williston State was still a high-risk campus but was doing its best.

With a business office that turned over multiple times and the phenomenal increase in business transactions, the college needed the chancellor's assistance to identify ways to mitigate the risks.

Shirvani said nothing of the college's efforts. He made no comments on the challenges facing the college. Instead, he expressed displeasure at the lack of doctorates on campus. You could hear a pin drop.

After an uncomfortable moment of silence, staff responded by talking about the college's inability to hire custodians, finance personnel, and technical faculty. Shirvani would hear none of it. He continued to stress the importance of having doctorates. He recommended a starting wage of $80,000. The college would then be able to attract candidates.

My staff's jaws dropped. Starting faculty salaries for Williston State were under $40,000, a hard-fought and highly improbable increase of 33% over the past two years and there were so many other increases that we desperately needed but could not get, like lights for safety and wages for security personnel. Now we should expect to raise money for $80,000 doctoral professors while the current professors and staff continued to be priced out of local housing and subject to high administrative staff turnover, unlit parking lots, and skyrocketing local crime? I held my tongue.

University Control

Shirvani, enjoying the full support of the State Board, quickly took control of the university system. The president of the State Board sent an email to the presidents that all communication needed to go directly to the chancellor. The message was clear. Shirvani was in charge.

Shirvani made policy recommendations to limit the presidents' authority. He, not the board, would have sole authority to terminate university presidents. He assessed the colleges for an internal auditor position and a compliance position.

He set up the annual calendar. But he changed the meeting dates and times changed constantly, causing considerable confusion and unpredictability. I did not have an assistant and would clear and reschedule my calendar in order to accommodate the roller coaster schedule, which caused a huge tidal effect, impacting many other people, including the mayor, local CEOs as well as faculty and staff. It was classic tail-wagging-the-dog.

For those meetings he did keep, he consistently arrived late. Chancellor Goetz had purchased a video conferencing system to allow presidents to meet from remote locations like Williston. Abandoning the video conferencing system, Shirvani mandated that the presidents meet in person, which put me back under incredible time and driving pressures. While people in big cities lament one to two hour commute times, they often have access to public transportation where they can read, write, and get work done. Executives in urban areas often have a driver to make better use of their time. The one president in North Dakota who hired a driver got publicly ridiculed.

And so the combination of North Dakota's "can-and-should-do-yourself" kind of state combined with Shirvani's autocratic leadership style mandating in-person attendance despite the vastness of the state and the availability of alternatives, resulted in my spending even more time away from home and even more distant from Joyce's more basic struggles.

I was now making the four-hour one-way trip to Bismarck for meetings that would be changed or canceled. Only when a previously-scheduled visit from an out-of-state dignitary (the Commissioner from the Montana University System) to Williston State College conflicted with a date changed last minute by Shirvani did he reluctantly give permission for me to attend a Cabinet meeting over the phone. But these were the least of my problems.

Chancellor Interference

Kathleen Neset, from Tioga, was appointed to the board June 20, 2012. Neset, president of Neset Consulting Service, Inc., provided well site geologicand geosteering services to the oil industry. She earned a B.A. in Geology from Brown University and went to work as a seismologist in Michigan. She had formerly worked as a Tioga High School science teacher, a Tioga school board member, and a substitute business manager at Tioga High School. She managed well site geology and mudlogging crews throughout the Bakken and Northern Rockies regions.

Highly regarded in her field, Neset was a strong ally and representative of a growing oil economy. She was also a friend of the governor. A staunch backer of Shirvani, Neset had a strong relationship with the University of North Dakota. With Representative Skarphol and Neset in Tioga, the college had hoped Neset would become its second ally. No one expected what was about to occur.

Supported by Shirvani, the dean of UND'S engineering school proposed building an engineering school in Tioga. Tioga, 49 miles from Williston, was the second largest city in Williams County. The university system was incapable of supporting one college in the heart of the boom, and now Shirvani was proposing a $30 million campus with a $4.5 million annual operating cost. The new campus would sit in WSC's backyard.

I immediately called the Chancellor to express my concerns. What was the plan for Williston State? He assured me that there would be dollars available in the next session, and he was also very clear that when the university system received oil impact money, the money would be released through him.

I once again explained to him the special session funding awarded to Williston State, the need to continue security and counseling as well as the need to adjust wage-inflated salaries. He cut the call short, citing another meeting, and said he would call me back the next day. No call ever came.

The proposal to build a separate campus, to my incredible relief, would never gain traction. Unfortunately, I had upset the chancellor by indirectly challenging his authority. Consequences followed shortly after that.

Chancellor Interference 2

"More than 500 foreign students—from Thailand, Jamaica and about a dozen other countries—are staffing nearly every hotel, car wash and fast-food place in town, tending to the troops of roughnecks from the oilfields. 'Without them, I don't know what we'd do,' said Ward Koeser, mayor of this city of 16,000, citing long lines, slow service and limited hours at stores and restaurants before the students arrived."

—North Dakota Cities Draw Foreign Workers,
Wall Street Journal, June 28, 2012[42]

The contract with United Work and Travel, although difficult, brought diversity to the campus. The program provided revenue to support the bond payments for the new student residence hall, and we avoided safety issues related to allowing a building to set empty in a community with a large transient population housing.

At the request of the city of Williston, the college made a request for the continuation of the short-term international program to the new chancellor. When I did not hear from him after several days, I contacted the system's attorney. His response: "The matter is being reviewed." The college's decision to allow J1 Visa students to live in the otherwise unused Dickson Hall would quickly come to an end.

On September 10, 2012 and without discussing the matter with me, Shirvani sent a letter directing me to terminate the contract with United Work and Travel:

"After consultation with university counsel and based on serious concerns, I will not support renewal of this contract and ask you to end this arrangement as soon as possible. The ending date for this with United work and Travel is September 14. This contract has not served the interests of WSC students and there are risks and potential liability associated with the arrangement. Housing transient workers in a campus building in close proximity to WSC student housing and permitting those workers access to facilities design and intended for use by WSC students raises legitimate safety and security concerns. Continued occupancy of an ageing building previously determine to be unsuitable for student housing raises serious concerns. Finally, housing foreign workers was not intended when the legislature authorized bonds or appropriated public funds to build, maintain and operate the facilities."

I was surprised that Shirvani characterized the international students as foreign workers. The participants were students first. That being said, the directive was clear. I ended the contract.

The city formed a committee to consider options for Dickson Hall. Housing was at a premium and businesses were relying on short-term international workers. The city requested, and I gave permission to do an inspection of the building. The building passed without issue.

City officials and local legislators met with the chancellor to see if there was any flexibility in his decision. After the meeting, Senator Lyson said the chancellor would allow international students to return if liability was taken from the university system. The public reaction was highly positive. But Shirvani knew that the likelihood of the college not having responsibility for a building on campus was minimal to none.

The CEO of Mercy Medical Center emailed me: "If you can't use your old dorm to house foreign workers, would you be able to rent it to Mercy for a year? I'm guessing not, but I had to ask..."

As the city and the chancellor played tug-of-war, the college had to plan for the possibility of an empty building on campus. Closing Dickson Hall was not so simple. How would the college raise $250,000 to offset the demolition cost? More worrisome, would the lost revenue from Dickson Hall negatively impact the bond rating on the college's new residence hall?

We could not in good conscience leave Dickson Hall open, but an empty building in a transient community was dangerous. As a wait list existed for family housing, I consented to three families living in the building. It was not ideal and probably did not comply with Shirvani's directive. But it would serve as a short-term placeholder until money was found to demolish Dickson Hall.

Shirvani had taken a beating for closing Dickson Hall, so it was not a big surprise when the vice chancellor for finance, "on behalf of the university system" blessed the college's continued partnership with the Department of Transportation.

The news was bittersweet; we had been looking for a good reason to get out of the DMV. Our neighbor Watford City had to close their DMV office when they lost their last employee. McKenzie County's DMV lost $70,000. We faced the same challenges and dangers but the Department of Transportation was probably too much for the chancellor to take on after having to deal with city officials and local legislators over the closing of the international program. We would lose the Dickson Hall residents, income, and cultural exchange, which had not presented any financial or security issues, but we would continue a partnership with Department of Transportation which brought security risks and potential financial loss.

On Our Own

The day after the receipt of Shirvani's letter to close Dickson Hall, the Higher Learning Commission (the college's accrediting body) held a site visit exit interview with Williston State's senior staff:

"Williston State College is working under extreme circumstances within the community of Williston, North Dakota. The College is part of a rapidly growing oil production community with little or no regard to the current infrastructure of the small city. While the College leadership explained in the Systems Portfolio the oil expansion and economic conditions in the community, the Quality Checkup team members attest to the extreme difficulty of work and life in Williston. Because of the oil field inflation, the cost-of-living, available affordable housing, stress on college salaries, and the availability of basic resources the College significant outside-of-their influence challenges all this while the funding formula appears to have remained at the pre-oil field rate. The College Leadership, Faculty, Staff and Students deserve to be commended on their resiliency and determination in times of massive growth, constant change and extremely difficult "quality of life" concerns."

—Higher Learning Commission Visit to
Williston State College, September 18, 2012

As was the custom, the report from the site visit was presented to the chancellor. Again, he did not respond. The report was never forwarded from Shirvani to the State Board. I was unable to update the State Board as Shirvani had removed the agenda item which allowed the president's to update the Board on their respective colleges.

At the same time Shirvani was composing a letter to cease operations in Dickson Hall, the college was notified it had successfully secured two significant funding awards which would bring in $4.3 million over five years. Both grants combined were greater than the college's annual operating budget.

The college was determined to succeed despite the university system. It was a herculean effort on the part of an inexperienced and small staff, but no one should ever bet against North Dakotan ingenuity. I had worked at two prior colleges and had never seen a master plan completed, but in three years, Williston State finished not one but two master plans.

Streets were named, multiple buildings opened, and the recreation center was being built on campus. The new science center, pulled from the backburner and shepherded by Lance Olsen, finally opened and to rave reviews. The foundation held a groundbreaking to celebrate the first day of construction for their apartment building. The governor was the guest of honor. Shirvani was nowhere to be found.

Something spectacular was also happening in athletics. The college's hockey team won the national championship. The women's fastpitch softball team started their first season. Basketball, baseball, and hockey were coming off winning seasons.

I became president the same year as President Obama. In 2012 President Obama was elected to a second term. But my family weighed heavily on my mind. I was highly doubtful I would have another four years to give.

Thoughts of Leaving

Moving Williston State's campus forward while running interference between the college and the university system was wearing me down. Yes, my wife and family returned, but Joyce was miserable. I knew our marriage was falling apart. I was burning the candle at both ends and had very little left to give to family.

Events occurring at the school district due to overcrowding were now at our front door. Joyce had been attempting to get Julia into grade school for Fall 2012 to little avail. She sent me a terse email that Julia were put on a waiting list.

Joyce was told that, although we were walking distance from Rickard Elementary School, anyone wanting to attend the school would be part of a lottery. If Julia and Emma were not lucky in the lottery, they would attend an undesignated school.

She was distressed by the lack of information concerning a potential new school, new teachers, and the support that would be available. Williston did not have buses so another school meant we would have to drive the girls back and forth.

I was no longer sure if my family was staying or leaving. I knew Joyce was struggling to remain in Williston. I was close to a breaking point as I spent even more time away from home at required in-person meetings half the state away. Joyce moved into a separate bedroom in the house. I was no longer in a position where I would be able to keep both my family and my job, so I began the search for another presidency.

A college in Maine, York Community College, was looking for a president. The school was about the same size as Williston State and a stone's throw away from the ocean. I applied. After a phone interview, I was moved forward as a semi-finalist. I would be flying to Maine to interview.

Williston was growing. The university system was imploding. I was sitting on the wrong side of the chancellor. The funding provided to the college during the special session needed to be sustained. I could not do it all, and I was no longer sure I wanted to keep trying.

Chapter 8
ALLIANCE

"The population boom in Williston, N.D., has been a blessing and a curse... Williston, the fastest growing small city in America, is enjoying an oil boom and has seen its population double in the past two years."

—NPR, December 18, 2012[43]

GOVERNOR DALRYMPLE

Governor Dalrymple was a maverick in education reform. As lieutenant governor, he reworked the K-12 funding model to the benefit of the schools. Now, as governor, he set his aim higher. Dalrymple established a higher education funding model based on performance. In the new funding model, state dollars would be tied to students finishing courses with passing grades. The model worked when the economy affected all colleges equally. Under different circumstances, it was genius. Unfortunately, in a hyperinflation environment where students were being lured to the oil field by large salaries, the one-size-fits-all model would not meet the needs of a college like Williston State.

The university system fully backed the governor's model—regardless of the impact on Williston State. Shirvani went so far as to send a directive to the other presidents mandating them to support the funding model. Presidents were also warned not to request anything outside of the governor's funding model.

My hands were tied. I was debating whether to ask Shirvani for an exception, knowing full well the answer would be no. But before I could even make the request, something remarkable happened.

For the second time in my career, I was summoned to the governor's office. My first thought was, naturally, "What could I have done this time?" When I arrived, governor Dalrymple and Ron Rauschenberger, the governor's chief of staff greeted me. The governor had only one question: Would I support his proposed performance-based higher education funding model?

The governor appoints State Board members. My boss, the chancellor, reported to the State Board. Understanding and respecting the chain of command, I stated categorically and without any hesitation that I supported the governor's proposed funding model.

Governor Dalrymple, knowing the new model would not benefit Williston State instantly made a commitment. If I could secure House and Senate support, a feat he cautioned would be similar to Williston State's successful but unlikely special session funding bid a year earlier (an accomplishment which the governor called unprecedented), he would not stand in the college's way.

I was astounded. The governor of the state of North Dakota was paying more attention to and taking more action on Williston State than the State Board. I would still have to speak with the Shirvani, but I would bide my time and wait for the right opportunity.

Governor's Dinner

Two days after the meeting with Governor Dalrymple, the presidents and State Board were invited to a dinner at the governor's mansion. The 25 guests were seated at a head table and two round tables. To my surprise, I was sitting at the head table. Even more surprising, the governor sat at one end of the table, and I sat at the other end of the table. The chancellor sat in the middle.

Shirvani appeared perplexed by his seating position. He was not seated next to the governor, and the president of one of his smallest colleges was sitting at the head of the table. Just like the special session funding, just like my salary increase, Williston State was once again singled out. I used it as an opportunity.

After dinner, I explained to the chancellor that the governor called me into a meeting earlier to let me know that he understood Williston State would have to seek additional dollars at the legislative session. He also understood Williston State's request would conflict with his new funding model. If the legislature provided additional dollars for Williston State, the governor said he would sign off on the bill. Standing in the governor's living room, I shared the story as if Williston's request for additional funding was a done deal with the governor The chancellor paused. He told me I had a lot of work to do and then turned and walked away.

Housing

A plain, one-bedroom apartment in Williston, N.D., rents for $2,100 a month. For this price, you could rent a one-bedroom apartment in New York City. Williston is not New York City. There are 30,000 residents and one department store. The nearest city is two hours away. Rents are so high in Williston because the town is in the middle of an oil boom. Unemployment is below 1 percent, and workers are flooding into town.

—NPR, January 10, 2013[44]

Terry and I met with Governor about a week later to discuss the building of the foundation's apartment building. The meeting included the Governor's direct reports and heads of the various state agencies. We wanted to know if the apartment building on campus could support the state's housing needs for their oil patch employees.

All the state agencies were struggling to recruit and retain employees in the oil patch. The consensus of the group was that Williston State College Foundation should move forward and build a

64-bedroom apartment. Each agency would commit to a block of rooms.

—

LEGISLATIVE SESSION

"The average worker in the oil and gas sector here earns more than \$90,000 a year – a sum so large that it's pushed up incomes in non-oil sectors as well. The overwhelming majority of these oil jobs require a high school degree or less. The oil and gas workforce here has increased from 5,000 in 2005 to more than 30,000 today. The recession remains in their minds: Many hail from outside the state and are working grueling 80-hour-a-week shifts in hopes of earning enough money to save their homes elsewhere from foreclosure." [45]

Turnover in the finance office made it difficult if not impossible to address audit findings. As I started to put the finishing details on the college's legislative request, I had to make another round of changes in the business office so I could spend time in Bismarck.

Even with special session funding and bonuses, the college was not retaining finance employees. I asked the state auditor if he might come out and visit the campus and provide some guidance. He put his hand on my shoulder, smiled and said: "I've got the same issues with a number of state agencies out west. I'm sorry, but I can't help you."

The business office was overwhelmed. For two months, the office had received zero applications for the director of campus services. My initial thought was to take direct control of the finance office, but with the legislative session in play, there was no way I could do both jobs. I decided to take executive action and reorganize. I would double down on the business office.

In addition to the business office, I created a separate finance office with a chief finance officer. I had heard that Laurie Furuseth, an active supporter of the college, was selling her accounting firm. Laurie was highly regarded in the community; her husband served as the city's attorney and was also on the college's foundation board. I actively recruited her to become the college's chief finance officer.

I asked Lance Olsen, a friend of Laurie's, to pitch her on the job. Laurie's husband was on Terry's board, so Terry talked to Laurie next. Our tag-team persistence paid off. Although Laurie could only work one day a week until the sale of her firm went through, she was on board. High-caliber finance people were unobtainable in Williston, so the college was willing to wait; we just hoped we didn't have to wait too long.

Resignations were occurring weekly. Over the past year, the entire financial aid office resigned. The director for financial aid provided eight weeks' notice, so it was not a full-scale emergency... yet. A campus services security employee was terminated because he did not show up to work. He was working another job at the same time he was supposed to be on campus, an increasingly common occurrence. The college no longer had Saturday security coverage, so I added two campus security rounds to my own Saturday schedule. It was going to be a tough legislative session.

I provided a preview of my request legislative request at the State Board meeting. I went into detail on the challenges facing the college. No action was taken, no questions were asked, and there was no verbal support from the State Board. I chose to interpret no response as tacit consent. Meanwhile, I could feel the noose tighten around my neck.

The presidents began the legislative session with testimony to the Senate's Higher Education Committee. My message to the committee was simple: if the legislature embedded special session funding into the college's operational budget, subsequent enroll-ment growth over time would eventually balance out the additional funds. Williston State, through the enrollment growth, would realign itself to the governor's performance funding model within four to six years.

At one point, I held up the college's latest audit report. I had brought copies for any legislator wanting to see what was taking place at Williston, and what was likely to continue without the legislature's support. No one requested a copy.

When I finished my presentation to the Senate's Higher Education Committee, I could tell the members were surprised and maybe even taken aback by my candor. Three people from the floor immediately got up and shook my hand. Disturbingly, I was the only president that did not have questions asked by the committee. Was that a good thing? I didn't know. But I felt a little alarmed that my presentation had such an impact—and a little confused that there were no questions.

—

HIT LIST

"Raymond Nadolny, president of Williston State College, has lost more than 50 percent of his staff – custodians, directors and executive team members – who left to work for higher-paying employers such as the oil companies. To prevent more quitting, he promoted a secretary to a human resources director within three months, with a 50 percent salary increase, and he is considering a similar step again. 'I hired a secretary this week,' he said in an interview. 'Immediately, when a director's position came open, I thought *this could be a good fit*.' The college has 24 mobile homes, including some purchased from the Federal Emergency Management Agency, at its campus to house more than a tenth of its employees as it's building a

$10 million, 72-unit apartment building. The vacancy rate in Williston is reportedly below 1 percent, according to Federal Reserve Bank of Minneapolis in a July article on its website."

—Bloomberg, February 21, 2013[46]

Turmoil

With the new chancellor, turnover was impacting the university system office. Unlike the college's turnover, which was voluntary, the university system office turnover was forced. By the beginning of the legislative session, Shirvani had already significantly downsized his staff. The atmosphere in the university system office was both intimidating and hostile.

Over the past several years, I had made good friends in the university system office. When I was in Bismarck, I would stop and update Laura Glatt, the vice chancellor of finance on the college. In the evenings, I would go out with the Randall Thursby, chief information officer, Erika Lorenz, the assistant to the chancellor, and Bill Eggert, the system's auditor. By the end of the year, none of my colleagues would be working for the university system, except Laura Glatt (though not for lack of trying by the chancellor).

It seemed I too would be joining my friends in leaving the university system. Rumors of the chancellor's "president's hit list" began to circulate. The president at NDSCS told me there were five of the eleven university presidents on the list although no one was quite sure which they were. On hearing the rumor, I immediately assumed I made the list. The chancellor's assistant confirmed my suspicion. She was also being forced out and would be one of the first staff members to take an early exit.

Three board members who were deeply invested in Shirvani's success were now running the State Board: Duaine Espegard, the Board president, Grant Shaft, the past president, and Kathleen Neset, the future president. I made a decision. I would ignore the alleged chancellor's "president's hit list" and get back to focusing on the college. If I got the boot, I got the boot. Until then, I had a legislative request to prepare.

Controversy

> The controversy over state university Chancellor Hamid Shirvani took a new turn Friday with Rep. Bob Skarphol grilling those he perceives as opponents of Shirvani. "I believe this whole controversy has been an absolute travesty," Skarphol said. "I am absolutely angry about it."
> —*Bismarck Tribune*, April 5, 2013

The issues facing the colleges took a back seat as the State Board spent more time on issues related to Shirvani. The animosity and tension between the college presidents and the chancellor began to surface in Chancellor's Cabinet. For six months, meetings were always rescheduled, Shirvani never arrived on time, and when the meetings did take place, the presidents were silent.

Shirvani then became involved in what would become the first of a string of controversies. The first involved the university system's new IT building located on the University of North Dakota's campus. Shirvani directed UND to create an office suite in the new building for when he was on campus. The president of the University of North Dakota rejected the plan.

Board members immediately came to the chancellor's rescue. The president of the State Board issued a press release noting Shirvani's efforts to be present at all of the system's colleges. It was in the same press release that I learned Shirvani had also requested to have an office in Williston. It was news to me. The chancellor had made no such request.

That same day, he caught up with me in the Capitol building. Shirvani was a rare sight at legislative hearings, so his presence was a surprise. His warm greeting was an even bigger surprise. Since the dinner at the governor's mansion, I had fallen on my sword, basically lowering myself to Shirvani to regain his trust. And, as the chancellor had allied himself to Representative Skarphol, I thought maybe I was being welcomed back into the fold. Neither was the case.

Shirvani asked if I could do him the favor of making an office available for his use on Williston State's campus. He said he understood how much the college was going through and he wanted to be in Williston as much as one day a week. Completely surprised at the total turnaround as he had not been on campus since the previous year and then only that single time, I agreed even though there was no room on campus. As he turned to walk away, he reminded me that he had made the request earlier. I nodded my head in empathy for his situation, not agreement. There had never been a prior discussion, only the chancellor's need to protect himself.

Legislators began grumbling about Shirvani. Grumbling soon turned into action. Senator Tony Grindberg added an amendment to the university system's higher education bill to allow the State Board to buy out the chancellor's contract. With two years left on Shirvani's contract, the cost was estimated at $800,000.

Senator Grindberg stated: "In my opinion, Chancellor Shirvani's leadership style is in serious question and his methods of campus communication have created an environment of fear and retaliation. In my 20 years of legislative service, I have never experienced such strong widespread opinions of questionable leadership and mistrust." Senator Holmberg also challenged Shirvani as a "questionable" leader who had created "an environment of fear and retaliation."

The higher education bill also contained Shirvani's request to almost double the staff of the university system office. Shirvani was not from North Dakota, and he failed to understand the "volunteer" nature of the state. Like the proposed campus in Tioga, his request was going nowhere.

Representative Skarphol, representing the oil patch, was spending a lot of time defending Shirvani. Three state board members came to the chancellor's defense, identifying attempts to remove Shirvani as nothing more than personal attacks. And the presidents were blamed.

On February 26, an amendment to provide the funding necessary for the State Board of Higher Education to buy out the contract of university system Chancellor Hamid Shirvani failed by a single vote. The very next day, the North Dakota State Senate reversed the vote from the previous day and approved the funding for the buyout. The bill still had to be passed by both floors, but the level of legislative attention was unprecedented.

Matters came even more dire for both the State Board and the chancellor. An allegation was made that the State Board was violating the state's open meeting laws. After Shirvani's scheduler had been pressured out, the university system found itself with no one keeping track of the state's public meeting requirements. North Dakota's attorney general announced an investigation.

The conflict between the chancellor and legislators further polarized the university system and the legislature. An even larger number of open record requests were being made to the university system on behalf of both legislators and the media. Although North Dakota was enjoying incredible economic prosperity, what everyone was talking about was the dysfunctional university system.

A new bill involving higher education was being floated in the senate appropriations committee that would eliminate the State Board. The bill didn't pass, but it did become the starting point for what would later become a constitutional ballot measure.

The conflict between Shirvani and the presidents had now reached its boiling point. Several presidents encouraged their respective faculty senates, staff senates, and student senates to speak out against the chancellor's leadership. The President of Minot State University, angered by Shirvani's three-tier plan, was sending incendiary emails to the presidents encouraging them to speak out on the chancellor's abuses. Senator Grindberg now openly discussed Shirvani's "hit list."

On March 21, The State Board of Higher Education passed a

resolution of "full support" for Shirvani. The final straw came shortly after when Ellen Chaffee, a former NDUS president, sent a complaint to the Higher Learning Commission.

Complaint

"This guiding value strongly emphasizes that the governing board must focus on the well-being of the institution...This complaint points out that the board has allowed itself to be systematically cut off from direct contact with the institutions and their presidents. Few board meetings take place on campuses other than the one in Bismarck, and the new protocol eliminated long-standing social and presentation occasions that gave host-campus personnel opportunities to talk with board members. The board's sole source of direct information has become the system chancellor. The chancellor has very little knowledge of any of the institutions and shows very little interest in learning more. He has fired or marginalized all of the veteran system office staff members and several have resigned. He does not demonstrate knowledge of state/national conditions or academic policy, and he often behaves unprofessionally."
—Ellen Chaffee Letter to Higher Learning Commission

In April, 2013, Ellen Chaffee, sent a letter of complaint to the Higher Learning Commission. Although the letter would not be addressed for another month, the ground beneath the university system was shaking. Multiple defections were taking place from the university system office. Both Bill Eggert, the university system auditor, and Josh Riedy, the system's chief information officer, resigned.

The State Student Council called a meeting in Bismarck to discuss a no-confidence vote in Chancellor Shirvani. Williston State students were confused due to being so far away from the politics of the university system. Because they had no idea how to vote if a no-confidence vote on the Chancellor was brought forward, they requested my counsel.

I shared with the students the challenges currently being faced by an oil patch college. Bottom line: The college had more urgent concerns. So, on February 23, 2013, the North Dakota Student Association, representing 48,000 university students, and with only Williston State's student government abstaining, passed a no-confidence vote on Chancellor Shirvani.

With a civil war waging in the university system and the university system office not speaking to legislators, the college presidents concluded their final presentation to the House appropriations committee. Surprisingly, the presentations went well given that both presidents and legislators appeared distracted by the drama taking place between the State Board and the Chancellor.

Interview

As I grew closer to my semi-final interview for the presidency in Maine, I started to feel guilty at the thought of abandoning the college. If I left for the interview knowing what hung in the balance for Williston State, wouldn't I be part of the abuse like all the others fleeing for greener pastures? Plus, the interview felt like a dirty secret. I had to make excuses to miss the men's participation in the national hockey championship tournament in New York. Yet, I was worn out by having to work the legislature with zero university support, and I was afraid of losing my family.

In the end, I traveled to Maine for a semi-final interview which proved to be successful. While the men's hockey team became national champions, I moved forward as a finalist for the presidency at York County Community College. But I was worried about leaving a fragile and vulnerable community in a lurch.

By the end of March, oil revenue was going through the roof, so there was a feeling of generosity around one-time projects. The potential generosity of the legislature was good news as Williston had two major projects on the list: renovation of Stevens Hall and the creation of a front drive.

As the legislative session was wrapping up, I became the only president to attend committee meetings. Rarely did I see anyone from the Capitol-based university systems office participate. Several legislators asked me if it was true that Shirvani had banned the presidents from attending these meetings and I explained I had heard of no such ban. My response appeared hollow in the wake of absent university presidents.

Under the previous chancellors, Laura Glatt, the vice chancellor of finance had served as the voice of the university system. Laura also took the time to send legislative committee progress reports to both the university system business council and presidents. I now found myself attending committee meetings, taking notes, and sending them to Laura who, using results posted on the legislature's website and my notes, continued to send updates to the presidents.

My friend and mentor Representative Skarphol was now knee deep in the Shirvani controversy. Standing up for Shirvani, Skarphol openly fought with State Board members as well as members of his management circle. Representative Skarphol would find himself crossing a line. He would eventually end his relationship with the inner circle and, in time, surrender any power he held.

At the Capitol, I found myself becoming more and more isolated. Legislators were angry at higher education. As I was the only college president attending committee meetings, I became a focus for legislators growing resentment with Shirvani. Legislators were also frustrated by the funding requests from the oil counties, worried about giving them too much. I was the Oil Patch President, I was in the crosshairs, and I was alone. Skarphol was nowhere to be found. When not in committee meetings, he remained behind closed doors fighting with his fellow legislators in a bid to protect Shirvani.

On April 4, 2013, I flew to Maine for my final interview at York County Community College. I scheduled the interview for Saturday so that I would not miss the most critical time of the legislative session. I was one of three finalists. On my arrival, I was told one of the candidates had withdrawn. It was now down to two.

I became increasingly conflicted about my application. The appropriations committee had not decided on whether to embed the two to three million dollars requested by the college. I became concerned legislators would find out I was a finalist for another job. Legislators would definitely find out if I were selected president. In that scenario, they might not take the college's request seriously. Given the timing, I withdrew my application.

When the other candidate was not selected as president, I realized the position would have been mine. But there was nothing I could do. My conscience would not allow me to abandon Williston State. I spent eight years of my life studying for the priesthood. Day after day, we focused on service to the community with our families being a distance second. My training kicked in; the college was standing on a ledge and I needed to protect my community and college, even at a cost to me personally.

I did not realize the gravity of the sacrifice I was making at the time. I didn't even consider how isolated Joyce had become and what this latest step backward would do to us. Maybe, I didn't even understand the consequences of my decision. I had placed work above family. I was not a priest. I was a husband and father. Karma would catch up to me.

As I guessed, within a week of my return from Maine, the college would learn whether the legislature included Williston State's request for additional assistance. Legislative conference committees began to meet, and all the bills would soon be finalized. With the controversy surrounding Shirvani, the university system had shut down. There was no support coming out of the system office. I had no choice but to attend the conference committee meetings and hoped that with my presence legislative leadership would not leave Williston State high and dry.

—

SPOILS OF WAR

Five months into the session, legislators were tired, if not burned out. The conference committee for the higher education bill was miserable for all those attending. Legislators just wanted to "get out of Dodge." Although Republicans controlled both houses, the animosity between the House and Senate was as intense as the animosity between the university system and the legislature.

The higher education conference committee would decide the fate of the State's one billion dollar plus higher education biennium budget. Representative Skarphol led from the House side. Senator Holmberg led from the Senate side. Again, I was the lone president attending. Knowing when the conference committee met was not easy. Most meetings were not posted until a day or even hours before they happened, so being in Bismarck was a must.

Skarphol came to the meetings angry. In his constant defending of Shirvani, he was alienating himself from Representative Carlson and his fellow representatives on the committee. Even though most of what occurred in conference committee was semi-scripted in advance by Holmberg and Skarphol (via Carlson), Skarphol in his anger and to the frustration of his House colleagues (and to the delight of Holmberg), went off script. Skarphol made it clear to the committee that no decisions would be made without first consulting Representative Carlson, Senator Holmberg's counterpart in the House. Skarphol stated the unspoken truth publicly: While Holmberg was the senate's gatekeeper, Skarphol was just a glorified errand boy for Carlson. Carlson owned and controlled both what went into and came out of the House.

As the conference committee drama unfolded, I took a seat in the back row. Each day, I made it a point to sit closer and closer to the front. By the last day, I sat in the first row. I paid attention and made sure that my active listening made a positive impression on the members of the committee. Since so few people attended the meeting, I was hoping my presence would remind Skarphol of the college and its needs. But at this point, I was not sure if Skarphol was able to do anything. By throwing his lot in with Shirvani, Skarphol had effectively neutered himself.

On the last day the conference committee met, frustration turned to surrender for Skarphol. The colleges received everything they had asked for, and the chancellor did not. Not only did the Chancellor not receive his additional staff, but his budget was also cut. The very last action of the committee and any remaining shred of influence Skarphol held went to Williston State.

Senator Holmberg begrudgingly added two million dollars to Williston State's base budget. Governor Dalrymple's performance funding model, which had passed earlier, now had a wrinkle. While the additional dollars kept Williston State afloat, the college would endure the ire of both the Legislature and other colleges for the next several years.

Senator Holmberg's parting comment to me was "Well, Dr. Nadolny. I guess you can bring the Brinks truck up to the Capitol, load your money, and go home." He was not happy with the disruption to the Governor's funding model—it was never supposed to happen.

On returning to Williston, I was again greeted with a reception worthy of a hero. The foundation presented me with a belt buckle inscribed with: "Dr. Raymond Nadolny, Thank you for bringing home the bacon." The appropriation was good news indeed. But like all things Williston, money would not solve all the problems. And with my dropping out of the Maine presidential search and my prolonged absence from my family while I fought in Bismarck for our college and community, I had made a complete mess of my family.

Chapter 9
BANKRUPT

Men (and a few women) from all over the country are descending upon the area to try and strike it rich. They've heard of $100K jobs for 22-year-olds with no experience, a 1 percent unemployment rate (compared to the national 7.5 percent) and people making more money than they know what to do with. What was once a sleepy region with large swaths of open space and tiny single-street towns has been inundated with thousands of workers, dozens of temporary housing camps, traffic, crime, and skyrocketing living costs.

—*The Fiscal Times*, June 6, 2013[47]

AN ILL WIND

I walked away from a promising job in Maine. My family was still together but only in the sense that we lived in the same house. Similar to "football widows," Joyce probably felt like a college widow. And so she continued to do her best, but largely without me. She decided to take the girls to Costa Rica to participate in a summer Spanish immersion program. I would again miss out on Julia's birthday and spend Father's Day alone. I wasn't sure if I was delaying the inevitable or even if I had a choice in the matter. But I consented to the family going to Costa Rica. I was miserable. The consequences of my decision to step out of the running for the Maine presidency were only just starting.

Pay Out

"The State Board of Higher Education voted Monday to remove Chancellor Hamid Shirvani, buying him out of his three-year contract. Shirvani will receive his salary, benefits and retirement over the next two years. Based on Shirvani's annual salary of $349,000 a year, plus scheduled pay raises, and planned retirement contributions, he will be due more than $800,000 for the remainder of his contract, not including health benefits. The University System didn't have the exact value of the buyout available Monday."

—*Grand Forks Herald*, June 3, 2013[48]

In an unexpected move, the State Board voted to buy out Chancellor Shirvani's contract in their June 2013 meeting. The university system must have been sitting on some cash, as the actual cost of the buyout was more than one million dollars. The buyout of Shirvani's contract also demonstrated a significant rift within the State Board. Board members Shaft, Espegard, and Neset were furious. The presidents were seen as instigators, and angry board members were looking to hold the presidents accountable for the chancellor's downfall.

So, in a bizarre twist, Shirvani was given two weeks by the Board to wrap up several projects. He was not going to leave quietly. The most important and controversial project was Shirvani's year-end evaluations of the presidents.

Several presidents (North Dakota State University, University of North Dakota, North Dakota State College of Science and Minot State University) received scathing evaluations from the departing chancellor. Shirvani's criticism of Dr. Fuller, President of Minot State University was especially sharp: "My overall sense is that you have exercised a form of myopic leadership that has probably served you well among certain elements in Minot but reinforced among your peers a growing exasperation due to your sense of exceptionalism for

Minot State University and your clear lack of respect for your sister institutions."

Fuller was enraged. Retiring at the end of the year, he didn't hold back: "I'm angry. I think this thing is an absolute joke."

All the evaluations were made public through multiple public information requests. My assessment by Shirvani was completely unexpected. I received high praise: "I know that this past year has been difficult for you and your senior staff. Nonetheless, I want you to know how much I have admired your tenacity and your dedication to the needs of the campus." While I was surprised by my evaluation, many of my colleagues were fuming.

The State Board entertained considerable discussion on whether to accept Shirvani's evaluations of the presidents. The MSU president made an impassioned plea to reject them. In the end, the State Board set the evaluations aside.

Larry Skogen, a colleague and the president of Bismarck State College, was selected as Interim Chancellor. Regardless of events that would occur later, Larry was the right person at the right time. Retired from a career in the Air Force, Larry was well-respected both in and outside of education circles.

Larry's job would not be easy. His primary task was the upcoming vote on the constitutional measure to eliminate the State Board. Williston State, once again, did not make the list of priorities.

Public information requests continued to inundate the university system. New open records requests included the presidents' personal emails. With eleven colleges scattered across a large state, email had been the preferred mode of communication. The number of public information requests, in addition to the scrutiny being received by the college presidents, ended our use of this once popular communication tool. Communication decreased significantly.

And if matters couldn't get any worse for the university system, they did. On July 28, the university system received a letter from the Higher Learning Commission of a required advisory visit that would bring peer reviewers to meet with state board members, university system staff, and the presidents. The visit would be the first time in history an accrediting agency investigated a university system. The State Board was now preoccupied with an impending accreditation visit, an upcoming vote on a constitutional measure to eliminate the state board and yet another change in the university system's leadership.

Lending a Hand

Williston State fared well in the legislative session. But the boom was taking a toll on some of the neighboring colleges. Fort Berthold Community College, chartered by the Three Affiliated Tribes, was in danger of losing their accreditation. As such, the school asked Williston State to take over their nursing program until the Higher Learning Commission completed their accreditation review.

I initially said no but faculty convinced me to change my mind. Instruction argued that the college would have the program for no more than a year. Furthermore, there would be no cost to the college. Since Williston State introduced the nursing program at Fort Berthold, we were in the best position to manage the program. Williston State was still in way over its head. I would cover my bases and ask permission from the interim chancellor.

Things in university system office were indeed changing. Larry approved Williston State's taking over the nursing program at Fort Berthold Community College. He was aware of the health care needs at the Fort Berthold Reservation. He also knew that the Fort Berthold nursing program was a critical piece in addressing them.

Williston State College had now taken responsibility for two foundation apartments, a recreation center, a DMV, and now the Fort Berthold Nursing program. To this day, I do not know what I was thinking. The college's commitment to the Fort Berthold Nursing program would extend to two, then three years.

Calm Before the Storm

"The way some see it, landing a job in oil-rich North Dakota these days carries only one requirement: a pulse. It may be true that almost any functioning adult without a long criminal rap sheet can probably land a job in a place where Walmart is offering jobs at $15 an hour and some Dairy Queens close one day a week because they can't fill employee shifts."

—*Rapid City Journal*, May 6, 2013[49]

Challenges continued to emerge, but with the special funding embedded in its budget, the college felt like it was once again in control. In fact, despite everything that had been thrown its way, Williston State appeared to be on a roll.

Washington Monthly named Williston State the 18th best community college in the nation. The new apartment building opened its doors. The finished campus drive project transformed the look of the campus, and the renovation of Stevens Hall would follow shortly on its heels.

While from the outside, Williston State may have looked like it was doing well with the addition of two million dollars in base funding, I knew otherwise. The college had lost its champion in Representative Skarphol as he retreated to his home in Arizona, the university system was in self-preservation mode, and, college turnover now exceeded 40%.

The college continued to operate like a MASH unit. Even with additional dollars committed to staff salaries, turnover continued unabated. As the college became increasingly desperate for employees, personnel issues increased dramatically. With an impending university system accreditation visit and internal university system office turmoil, the system had new reasons to place WSC on the backburner. This may have been why the Chancellor did not jump when I called him with the bad news.

—

BROKE

"Everyone has heard stories about the shale-oil boom towns that are transforming North Dakota, for better and worse. 'Man camps' for oil-field workers, jobs for anyone who can work a rig or drive a truck, social distortions like those of the Klondike. You know the stories, and the town of Williston ND (where we've not yet visited, but plan to)…"

—*The Atlantic*, September 8, 2013

On August 30th, the President of the Bank of North Dakota called to inform me that the college had insufficient funds. I grew pale and had a temporary out of body experience. I told him I would take care of the situation immediately. He thanked me and said the bank would cover the college's outstanding checks.

When I got off the phone, I was trembling. The situation was a nightmare. The college was overdrawn by $500,000. Worse, the college had been periodically overdrawn over the past six months.

Regardless of the reason, I was responsible. I would call the interim chancellor immediately. I would get fired, but I was ready to accept the consequences.

To my surprise, Larry did not fire me. In fact, he let me know that I was doing a great job and he was sure I could take care of the matter. I was in shock.

Running out of cash was by far the biggest blow faced by the college to date. How could it have happened? Why wasn't I fired? Why wasn't a university SWAT team sent in to make the corrections?

My first thought, unlike Larry's, was to fire the Vice President of Business Services. But his inexperience was part of the risk I'd assumed in hiring him. Plus, steps were already being taken to create a separate finance office. Now was not the time to make further changes; this was the time to learn what caused the current problem.

In one hour, I uncovered why the college had gone into arrears. The Financial Aid Director, six months on the job and formerly the

Assistant to the Vice President for Instruction, had not billed the foundation for $235K in scholarships awarded to students over the past spring and which the foundation was committed to paying. This major A/R oversight was just the tip of the iceberg.

Success is its Own Worst Enemy

A hiring freeze of all unfilled positions was immediately put into place. Until I could see improvement, I would sign off on ALL college expenditures. Financial aid was tasked with getting a handle on revenue owed. Academic Affairs needed to review expenditures, revenue reimbursed, and revenue owed relating to the two federal grants. I requested additional assurances that the partnership with Fort Berthold would not result in a financial drain on the college.

By the time the cabinet met the next day, multiple factors impacting the cash balances had been identified. Unlike Financial Aid's billing issues with the foundation office, most of the factors were related to the college's success combined with its lack of a reserve. TrainND growth, unbilled scholarships to the Foundation, and the two grant awards were the primary culprits.

Over the past four years, TrainND had grown from serving 3,000 workers annually to nearly 18,000. We did not realize that with the increase in business contracts, there was also an increase in the number of outstanding payments to the college. Oil companies were notorious for paying bills late, and TrainND had $800,000 in uncollected bills.

The college was also bleeding cash from its two grant awards. Both grants, worth millions to the college, were reimbursed quarterly. Only after the expenses were made could the college get reimbursed. As we had no reserves, the numerous deficits in uncollected revenue added up to a college severely depleted of cash.

Finally, I discovered that the college's business office had changed the schedule for drawing down money from the state. The new timetable had the college receiving twelve equal payments.

Williston State was now the only college drawing down equal amounts over each of the twelve months of the year. Staying with the old schedule where dollars were frontloaded could have diverted the cash crises.

Another Scare

The Vice President of Business Services walked into my office unannounced. He claimed to have discovered the source of the college's negative cash balances. The current cash problems were not caused by unbilled scholarships, unrecovered funds from the Federal grants, or TrainND's uncollected payments of $800,000. Rather, the college had overspent on the residence hall by almost two million dollars.

By this point, I had learned not to jump out of my skin when presented with bad news. Indeed, bad news seemed to be a weekly (if not a daily) experience given the number of new employees on staff. In a worst-case scenario, if the VP were right, the college, already with no cash reserves, would be short millions, not just $500,000. In the best-case scenario, he was wrong, and the college still had to address the current shortfall in cash.

I was not about to cry wolf—at least, not yet. I calmly told the VP to check again and be 100% sure that two million dollars had been overspent on the new residence hall. The next day, he called me back saying the residence hall accounts balanced. Between new employees and inexperienced employees, I was right in not jumping the gun. I had kept my cool but lost another night's sleep.

As the new CFO would begin working full-time starting November 1, I immediately made the request for the state to allocate more dollars upfront. But the additional dollars would not be available until January. So the college needed to scrutinize expenses for two more months until a substantial cash buffer was in place.

Once again, I was astounded how many times life could do a 180° in Williston. A month earlier, the college was ranked as the 18th best community college in the nation, had the lowest tuition in the state, received an additional two million dollars in operational funding from the legislature, and was recording record breaking enrollment. But with one call from the BND president, all the accomplishments were forgotten. The cash crisis became another bump in what had become an epic Williston adventure.

Higher Learning Commission Letter

While the college was knee deep in red ink, the university system was busy preparing a response to the Higher Learning Commission (HLC) letter. Tasked with accrediting individual colleges, the HLC was charting new ground with its decision to investigate the North Dakota University System.

The HLC questioned whether the state board was providing adequate oversight and governance to North Dakota's 11 public higher education institutions. There was no doubt in my mind that one board could not adequately govern eleven separate institutions. State Board members, on the other hand, thought the problem stemmed from a lack of central control, while legislators like Representative Skarphol wanted greater accountability from presidents. Add increased enrollment demands in a state with decades of declining population, and one might have easily predicted the HLC visit.

The university system was preparing for a response as though their very existence depended on the outcome. It did. The Interim Chancellor created a new chief of staff position. Murray Sagsveen was named Chief of Staff, Ethics Officer, and Director of Legal Services for the university system. Sagsveen retired as a brigadier general and served as the senior judge advocate in the Army National Guard in 1996. He was recalled to the National Guard in 2011 to respond to the flooding in Minot. Sagsveen was well known in the state with 17 years of service in a law practice. He had impeccable credentials. He would have the additional responsibility of consolidating the university system legal team. The eight attorneys, under Sagsveen's supervision, would ensure that the university system remained in compliance with open meeting laws, amongst other activities. Between Larry and Murray, the university system was turning itself around.

Staying Focused

The college was not in a position to be distracted by the drama being played out in the university system. We needed to stay focused on the problems at hand. Negative cash balances had everyone operating at a heightened level of stress.

Fortunately, when the college released its official fall 2013 census data. Headcount was up. In a state of artificial and declining enrollment, an 11% increase was dramatic. The college and the foundation also celebrated the grand opening of the apartment complex and the front drive; the Governor attended both events and commented that, for the first time, the college looked like a real campus. Even with the Governor's praise, I had a bad feeling. It seemed that every time something good happened, something equally bad followed. I am not superstitious by nature. But it would not be inaccurate to say that I was starting to feel cursed.

Second Call from Bank of North Dakota President

A couple of days before Halloween, I received a second call from the President of the Bank of North Dakota (BND). The college had made up the $500,000 in missing cash but had once again overspent the checking account. I shared with BND's president the college's work to date. He sounded confident.

Again, expecting to be fired, I called the interim chancellor and updated him. Larry once again expressed his confidence that I would take care of the college's cash issues. The last thing a university system under review by the Higher Learning Commission needed was a finance scandal by one of its institutions. In other words, the college was again on its own.

The new CFO, Laurie would be working full-time in a matter of days. I could see the light at the end of the tunnel. But because of this latest call, I was on high alert over the college's cash balances. Every morning, besides doing a review of expenditures, I was now doing a daily review of the cash balances in the college's six bank accounts. Spending slowed significantly.

I decided to take a hands-on approach with financial aid. I walked down to the financial aid office and explained the gravity of the financial situation. Within 24-hours, an invoice was created for the nearly $500,000 in outstanding foundation scholarship awards. I walked the invoice over to the foundation. Terry's response to receiving the bill: "It's about damn time."

By the end of November, we had made significant progress. The total cash in all of the college's accounts was $682,000. Whether the college would keep solvent until January 1, 2014, was still unknown. A major bond payment for the residence hall was also due before year's end.

Family Reunion

Costa Rica was a tremendous success. The two youngest girls and Joyce returned from Costa Rica conversant in Spanish. Our reunion, however, was anything but joyful. It was clear that my family had one foot out the door, and Joyce openly talked about separation. I promised Joyce I would begin my search again. This time, there would be no backing out.

I began the tedious process of applying for two presidencies in Pennsylvania. Both colleges were driving distance from my in-laws. Both colleges were like Williston State but without the drama.

With dire fiscal straits at the college, additional time spent making applications for another presidency, and discussions of separation, I found myself on edge. In a short period, I had gone from college cheerleader to college troll.

I was living in Williston. I should have known that the well was deep. What was even more concerning: there was still a long, long way to go before I hit bottom.

—

ASSAULT

"Now, six years later, the region displays all the classic contemporary markers of hell: toxic flames that burn around the clock; ink-black smoke billowing from 18-wheelers; intermittent explosions caused by lightning striking the super-conductive wastewater tanks that hydraulic fracturing makes a necessity; a massive Walmart; an abundance of meth, crack, and liquor; freezing winters; rents higher than Manhattan; and far, far too many men. To oil companies, however, the field is hallowed ground, one of the few in history to break the million-barrel-a-day benchmark, earning it 'a place in the small pantheon of truly elite oil fields,' as one Reuters market analyst wrote."

—*Grist*, October 14, 2014[50]

Just when I thought nothing could be worse than a bankrupted college, tragedy struck again. An allegation of rape was made against several members of the Williston State hockey team. My priorities shot back into perspective. Regardless of the college's financial situation, the job was about students.

On Nov 17th, Williston State College was made aware of a charge of sexual assault: forcible rape reported to have occurred between the hours of 1 a.m. and 5 a.m. on Friday, November 15th. The alleged sexual assault took place in the college's residence hall involving individuals known to the victim, and the investigation was ongoing.

The allegation involved five members of the men's hockey team, which at the time was well placed to win a second national hockey championship. Discipline problems with the hockey team had increased since winning the national championship the year before—which meant the allegation was, at the very least, alarming.

No one on campus, including myself, had the experience to deal with the current allegations. The claims would be reviewed under Title IX guidelines, which had recently been tightened by the federal government. Multiple campuses across the country were now under scrutiny for lax processes regarding sexual misconduct and discrimination under Title IX.

A typical investigation lasted 60 calendar days following receipt of the complaint. It was a real possibility that the alleged incident would be picked up by the newspaper. For the third time in three months, I picked up the phone to call Larry and inform him of yet another problem. Once again, he expressed his complete trust in me. I couldn't help but ask Terry: "What does it take to be noticed out here? In fact, what does it take to be fired?" He didn't have an answer for me.

As the college did not have a Title IX officer, I met with the Executive Director of Student Services, the Athletic Director, the hockey coach, and the counselor and formulated a plan. The hockey coach would meet with the students in question and would follow up with them from our earlier discussion. Until the investigation concluded and a determination of charges was made, all players involved would be suspended from the team.

As advised by the police department, the hockey coach would advise all players to notify their parents and prepare them for what may lie ahead. The lead detective also communicated that all players should remain in Williston. Kirsten Franzen, the University System Compliance Officer, would come out in early December to start the administrative review of the alleged incident.

For two months before the rape allegation, I slept little out of concern for the college's finances. I worried endlessly, feeling like the carpet could be pulled out from underneath me at any moment. Now, the allegations against the school's hockey players provided me with a new perspective. Whenever I felt concern, worry or anxiety about the college finances, I would make myself focus on the alleged sexual assault. Any stress over the college's finances quickly diminished. If I began to panic over the alleged sexual assault, I would turn my attention back to the college's finances. Any stress over the alleged sexual assault diminished, but not as quickly. Contrasting two horrible incidents became balancing points that allowed me to keep my focus, my wits, and my sanity. I was not proud of the method, but it did help me in addressing two significantly different traumas.

On December 4, the police investigation wrapped. None of the players would be charged. Cameras from the hallway showed one female and five males enter a room in the residence hall. All had been drinking. It did not appear from the video that the woman was forced into the room. It did not appear from the video that the woman was distraught on leaving. Ultimately, the incident came down to what she said took place in the room versus what the men said happened.

An internal investigation still had to be completed and would start the following Monday when the compliance officer came to campus. With the lack of police charges, the male students were allowed back on campus. Having the compliance officer for the university system conduct the investigation felt good. It was an appropriate arms-distant relationship.

—

BABY BOOM

"The epicenter of the nation's energy boom is the Bakken. And evidence exists to suggest a possibly louder and maybe even more-welcome boom than the oil boom: the Baby Boom. Over the past year, 12 percent of Williston State University employees went on maternity leave. The baby boom, like the oil boom, is changing the way we live and work. A decade ago, Mercy Medical could expect anywhere from 200 to 300 births in any given year. Today, 100 births are projected in November alone. In 2015, Mercy may reach as many as twelve hundred births. The baby boom is the latest development in understanding Williston's ranking as the fastest growing micropolitan city in the country (with populations between 10,000 and 50,000). Thanks in part to the baby boom, Williams County now has the country's largest decline in the average age of its population—1.6 years."

—'Baby Boom' Marks Latest Boom in Northwest N.D.,
July 4, 2014, *Grand Forks Herald*[51]

As the college emerged from fiscal insolvency, inflation and staff turnover would run rampant for one last time. But in 2014, something amazing happened, staff turnover was overshadowed by staff pregnancies. Some say life doesn't give you more than you can handle. Maybe they are right. Just when I thought the burden was too heavy to carry, the oil boom turned into a baby boom.

Marry Me

"I've always wanted to be a June Bride... and have a baby right off, in the spring maybe."

—*Seven Brides for Seven Brothers*

The rise in marriages was easily explainable. The majority of employees that came to work for the college were female in their early to late twenties. The oil boom economy increased the number of jobs with titles like "roughneck" and "roustabout." Those jobs involved hard manual labor, typically in a dangerous working environment, and were held predominantly by males.

An explosion in the male population, a dwindling number of females, and an increasing number of women either engaged or married created a risky environment for women even if one was engaged. Engagements became shorter and shorter as a decreasing female population became even smaller because of the marriage contract.

A predatory environment, the increasingly shortened engagements, the steep increase in employee marriages should have prepared us for what was about to take place. On top of forty percent employee turnover, twelve percent of Williston State employees would go on maternity leave. The baby boom, like the oil boom, was once again changing the way the college lived and worked.

When a child is ill in a family (10 times on average in a child's first year), it is typically the secondary wage earner who misses work to care for the child. Williston State College employees were primarily female, secondary wage earners. With little to no daycare, employees were burning through sick leave.

The baby boom even affected the college's senior leadership table. In the middle of one of the leadership meetings, I heard a soft cooing. Looking beyond the other end of the boardroom table, I could barely make out the handle of a stroller. The Executive Director of Student Affairs, Heather, lost her daycare for the day, and she came to work with her newborn in tow.

The college had to become extremely flexible in allowing employees to bring children to work. Some days, I was not sure if I was running a college or a daycare. The college launched a task force made up of new parents to provide guidance on ways to be more responsive and supportive in a baby boom workplace. What ultimately supported parents supported Williston State.

Survival

Dealing with constant turnover necessitated some out-of-the-box thinking. The college explored the feasibility of setting up a Williston State finance office at the University of North Dakota. Just as the oil industry placed management offices and other white collar jobs outside of Williston, the college would adopt a similar model. A nonverbal agreement was established with UND, and an office was assigned to a Williston State employee.

The college had now survived two close calls of near bankruptcy, an allegation of sexual assault, and was successfully dealing with forty percent turnover as well as twelve percent of its employees on maternity leave. The college looked like a campus. TrainND would soon break ground on a new training facility. I had made it as a finalist to not one, but both Pennsylvania presidential searches. I might very well be separated, but I was still married. I would continue to tough this out.

Chapter 10
ABANDONED[52]

"Men come to Williston from all kinds of places, far and near –
almost all of the migrants we see in "The Overnighters" are
male – but the majority are white working-class Americans
who couldn't earn a living wage wherever they came from...
Finding gainful employment in Williston is one thing; having
to live in what one disillusioned Wisconsinite describes as a
'shitty-ass place' is quite another."

—*Salon*, October 9, 2014[53]

REJECTED

I completed the first of two final interviews for president. The
meetings ran an entire day as I sat with student groups, faculty
groups, staff groups, the community, and lastly trustees. I exited the
final interview feeling fully confident that I was the college's next
president. I loved my visit and knew that if I got the offer, I would
accept. The feeling seemed reciprocal. One board member told me:
"You will be our next president."

When I didn't get the job, I was heartbroken. Meetings with
faculty, staff, and board members were highly enthusiastic. What
could have happened? One final interview at the second college
remained.

Again, I began with excellent interviews with students, faculty,
and staff. At the interview with the board, I could tell the members

were fully engaged, so I asked if they had any additional questions. I had opened Pandora's box.

Questions ranged from taking away American jobs (international student housing) to audits to strippers. I was stunned. I asked where the members received their information. A board member held up a stack of papers that looked like a large book: "The consultants do a media search and provide it to us."

I was working in North Dakota, a small state (and an open records state). Unlike Washington where presidents received little media coverage, North Dakota presidents get treated like TV reality stars. Working in Williston, the reality was mostly soap opera.

It all made sense. I was devastated. My reputation was smeared in the uncensored, and unregulated annals of social and digital media. I was also tired. The interviews had taken a lot of time and added more stress to an already stressful job. And now, I would most likely lose my family.

Given the surreal nature of the oil path, and regardless of my accomplishments, the Williston State reality show would always cast doubt on my professionalism and abilities. I had become damaged goods, and I wasn't quite sure my reputation could be repaired. I needn't have worried; my reputation had not even begun to suffer.

Alone

"I can only commend you for having the patience of Job when it comes to managing your financial affairs office. I'm reminded of the saying that a guy just can't catch a break. Each time you've moved to resolve the personnel issue in your financial affairs office, something else looms larger and recreates the old problems. I do compliment you, however, for working with UND and trying, at least, to hire remotely located personnel to fill an urgent need for financial affairs expertise... Lesser individuals would have quit, and no one would have blamed them. You have, however, continued, under the most stressed conditions possible, to resolve, to invent, to create, to accomplish."

—2013-2014 Interim Chancellor's Evaluation
of the Williston State College President

Joyce could wait no longer. We separated. We told the girls that Mom was going back to Seattle for work. My two older step-children would remain with me to finish high school. The two younger girls would return with Joyce and go back to school in Seattle.

I felt alone yet again. My wife and my two little girls were residing in Washington. My step daughters were home, but being in high school, I never saw them. Even if they had been home, I was rarely home. During the day, I worked as president and campus services director. At night, I did multiple security rounds on campus.

I would not be able to keep all these balls in the air for much longer. Too much was going on at the college and home. I was floundering. The boom was reaching its peak, and like fireworks on Fourth of July, it was saving the best for last.

Near the End

"A big part of all this building is to improve the quality of life in western North Dakota. So a number of major facilities have opened in recent years to do just that... And Williston opened a 236,000 square foot recreational center, with indoor courts, fields, and a swimming pool at a cost of $75 million... Back in 2011, Blake and I had to stay in an RV because there were no vacant hotel rooms... When booking travel this year, we passed on a room at the Hampton Inn and Suites in Williston for $269 a night."

—*CNN Money*, February 4, 2014

People started to question openly whether the boom was slowing. Population growth and job growth were slowing. No one was sure, but the level of frenzied activity seemed to be calming down. As the boom was going on five years, it was hard to believe that the end just might be in sight. We only had to wait another six months to find out. But until then, the ride was not quite over.

Once again I was called upon to live up to the volunteer tradition. The campus services director had resigned to start his own company and, since we received zero applications for the job, I took over campus services. As the Interim Campus Services Director, I faced a steep learning curve. I attended weekly meetings on the $12 million Stevens Hall renovation. I learned how to activate the sprinkler system. After work, I spent North Dakota's long daylight evening hours restriping the parking lot. If employees were expected to work multiple jobs, the president would lead by example.

Interim Director for Campus Security

As Interim Director of Campus Services, I was, by default, in charge of security. On my very first week, the contractor working on Stevens Hall reported the theft of numerous items, mostly tools. When I told the diesel instructor about the thefts, he informed me that all the batteries in the diesel program's semi-trucks had been removed. When I related the diesel instructor story to Terry Olson, he informed me that the construction manager for the new apartment building reported squatters living in the new apartment under construction. I had my hands full.

The city's police were still overwhelmed. I asked my daytime security officer to park the security vehicles at different spots on campus with lights flashing. Hopefully, the presence of the vehicles would be a deterrent.

We lost a second security officer when I discovered that he too was working a second job at the same time he was supposed to be working at the college. After a long search, a replacement was finally hired. There was just one problem: she was afraid of the dark. She would spend her shift sitting locked in her vehicle under one of the college's light poles. I was too overwhelmed and too short-staffed to do anything. As long as she drove the car from light pole to light pole, I would let it go, at least temporarily.

A second complaint was filed against her shortly thereafter. Apparently, she was bringing her middle-school-aged grandchild to work because her son did not have daycare, a common problem in Williston. We had no choice but to fire her. I was back to doing evening security detail.

Vigilance

Living across the street from the college in a home with large bay windows created additional difficulties. My eyes were always on the alert for traffic going in and out of the college. Whether entertaining guests at a party or just having family dinner, I was constantly excusing myself to check out unwelcome visitors on campus.

One night, I was entertaining Richard Stenberg, and his wife. It was on nights like these where Richard taught me pretty much everything I know about North Dakota history. While enjoying dinner, I noticed three men carrying black garbage bags back behind Stevens Hall and the Residence Hall. They were dumpster diving. I did not want to disturb my guests, so I continued with dinner making sure I kept track of the intruders' activities. Out of the corner of my eye, I caught a fourth person carrying a garbage bag coming out from a grove of trees from the back of campus. Time to act.

I excused my guests telling them I would be right back. Richard demanded to know where I was going so I told them. Richard was not going to let me go out alone and said he was accompanying me. I told him it was no problem as this happened frequently. I would call the police on my way out, meet the men and tell them that I had called the police and that they needed to leave campus before the police arrived (when and if the police arrived). Richard still insisted on going.

With Richard and I in pursuit, the men started to flee. As they did not move very fast, not willing to give up the garbage bag each was carrying, we caught up. Mary, Richard's wife, was watching events unfold from the house, growing worried. Richard and I told the men that the police were on their way and that they needed to collect their belongings from the woods and leave campus immediately. One individual became agitated and started to yell. I remained calm, I repeated that the police were on their way, and I then turned to Richard and told him it was time to leave. Fortunately, by the time we started to walk away, a patrol car drove up, and we directed the officer to the men. The officer escorted the men off campus.

I am sure Richard and Mary thought I was insane. But as I oversaw security, and when we were not able to hire an evening security officer, the responsibility fell on my shoulders. Living in a house across campus with a perfect sight of the college's front door made things easier. But the state of near constant vigilance only increased my stress levels to a point where I occasionally questioned my sanity. I was not alone in this regard. D'Wayne Johnson, a Tioga superintendent and respected colleague, was going through his own oil patch drama.

Afraid

D'Wayne Johnston, 49, had worked in education for more than 20 years. He had been with the Tioga school district for nine years, serving as the Tioga school superintendent for the past six years. The city of Tioga was only 40 miles from the college.

Kind and always professional, D'Wayne was also an alum of the college. His brilliant career, marked by a string of successes, was cut short. In fear for his life, D'Wayne brought a concealed weapon to school.

The school district was experiencing a lot of pressure because of the oil boom. The enrollment in Tioga had doubled in the past three years. The school was adjusting from being a small school where everyone knew each other to a large school with an increasingly transient population.

D'Wayne had a confrontation with a student with behavioral issues. Although the student was never identified, it was reported that the student had recently moved to Tioga with his family. The police had already been called once about the student's behavior. Behavior issues continued. When D'Wayne expelled him, the student responded with threats. The student allegedly made hand gestures pointing his finger as if he was shooting D'Wayne and the people standing around him.

Security precautions were being put into place. The school district had been in the process of installing security cameras and safety training for staff was in the works. There was still general concern over whether the school district could respond to an active shooter incident.

The chair of the school board had submitted testimony earlier in the year on a bill that would have allowed the school to appoint a representative to carry a concealed weapon. Representative Rust, the area's state representative in the House at the time and a retired Tioga school superintendent, supported the legislation but it ultimately failed. Rust, now a senator, believed that remote areas like Tioga, farther from law enforcement personnel, were not prepared for an active shooter incident.

D'Wayne was worried about the student's threats. He was not able to sleep. That worry soon turned into fear for the safety of his students and staff. The next day after the threats, D'Wayne carried a concealed handgun in a holster beneath his jacket to school. Someone at the school saw the weapon and made a complaint.

A gun-control group wanted his resignation. D'Wayne took direct responsibility for the incident. He acknowledged there was no justification for his actions. He knew he let the community down.

With one principal already on medical leave, D'Wayne was allowed to resign at the end of the school year.

The Executive Director of the North Dakota School Boards Association weighed in saying Johnston should have turned to the police. He was right. But from the safety of Bismarck, no one really understood the fear that comes from living in a transient community.

My paradigms for understanding the world were being turned on their head. I am against gaming. I am against exploiting women. But my foundation held the gaming contract in the local strip club. I am a fiscal conservative, but my campus depleted its funds multiple times. I had strong convictions about what a university should look like, yet I purchased multiple FEMA trailers. I am against guns. I would not allow security on campus to carry a weapon. But living in Williston, I empathized with D'Wayne.

There is no formal training for experiences like these. Mistakes get made. And in D'Wayne's case, one errant judgment now tarnished a brilliant career.

Besides resigning, D'Wayne was given a letter of reprimand that was placed in his file. Although it was an isolated incident in what had been a stellar career, his professional future was now questionable. A teacher to the end, D'Wayne hoped the incident would start a discussion on school safety in western North Dakota. Like most bad things in the Oil Patch, it was swept under the carpet and soon forgotten. I, however, couldn't shake the feeling that I was on the brink of my breaking point.

Burnout

"Up until Monday, I was in charge of campus services, capital projects, and did night-time security. My student services exec is doing double duty both as the director of financial aid. My marketing director is doing double duty as public information officer. My IT Director is doing double duty as network manager. My HR Director is a one-person office machine. My athletic director, who started two months ago, is managing seven coaches, five who are newer employees than him. My assistant also coaches our volleyball team, and has just finished being in charge of the College's summer landscaping. We are the only government agency without a significant backbone. The University System Office has no back bone and we are billed for everything. I have shared this with the Chancellor."

—2014 October Williston State Presentation to Governor's OMB

I needed to find someone to take over campus services and was ready to throw money at the problem. The new campus services director would be paid between $100,000 and $110,000. Still, not one good candidate crossed my desk.

With zero qualified applications, I finally made the decision to recruit a candidate on my own. I reached out to an old colleague I worked with at Cochise College in Arizona. At that time, Vince Pachuillo was the school's finance director, and I was the one reporting to him.

Vince had covered a lot of ground since we last worked together. He had gone on to work as a vice president in a developing African country. I thought that the crazy conditions in Williston could not be much different from a developing country.

Vince had moved back to the United States and was working in the finance department in a community college in Arizona. Fortunately for us, Vince consented to fly out for a visit. He accepted the job and would start in October. With the addition of Vince, I even had some backup for the finance area.

—

ONCE IN A LIFETIME

"Petrodollars can buy the finer things in life. And in one North Dakota oil county, they will be used to pay for the higher education of every graduate of area high schools, if students want."

—Foxbusiness.com, October 24, 2014[54]

"The Williston community has been affected by the oil boom in a lot of negative ways, but many bright spots have come because of the vast oil production. One of those came last month when Williston State College made one of its biggest announcements, offering free scholarships to all Williams County high school graduates, the Williston Herald reported."

—*The Crookston Times*, November 26, 2014[55]

Terry Olson, Williston State College Foundation Executive Director, was the hero that stepped forward once again. In the midst of chaos, something wonderful was about to happen. And it was not about oil. Between the Foundation, a private trust, and the state, the Williams County Scholarship was created. Every 2015-2016 high school graduate from the college's service area would be awarded a scholarship that covered tuition, fees, and books.

Free tuition was a growing topic in the nation. Senator Bernie Sanders was making free tuition a significant part of this 2016 presidential campaign platform. The university system was yet again too busy to take notice. Other colleges were concerned about declining enrollments and felt the scholarship would stop students in the Williston area from attending other North Dakota state colleges. While the scholarship was significant for northwest North Dakota, the university system, caught up in its attempt to defeat a constitutional measure to eliminate the state board of higher education, completely ignored this exceptional opportunity of national significance.

Undeterred, the college continued to advance. With the assistance of UND, the college had managed to get through the fall semester with a makeshift staff in financial aid. Laurie was slowly rebuilding the finance office and I was no longer checking the cash balances daily. Vince had come on board, relieving me of campus services. Only a couple of months remained before faculty and staff would return to Stevens Hall. It occurred to me that the college, despite the university system, might just survive the boom. I was now set up for the biggest surprise of my life.

Chapter 11
BULLIED

"For Supreme Court Justice Ruth Bader Ginsburg, falling asleep at the State of the Union address is nothing new. All it takes is a good glass of wine. As she did two years ago, Ginsburg admitted Thursday night that, yes, the photos of her appearing to nod off at President Obama's big speech last month showed her dozing."[56]

—*USA Today*, February 13, 2015

EVICTED

On October 15, 2015, a process server representing the North Dakota University System called me. He informed me that he needed to deliver a letter and asked where we could meet. He was also going to have to take any work keys in my possession as well as my college computer.

It was my first experience with a process server. I felt slightly alarmed, but working in the oil patch had taught me not to leap to conclusions or, for that matter, jump the gun. There would be plenty of time to worry. Not knowing the gravity of the situation, I did not want to meet the gentleman on campus, as I was not sure if he drove a marked car or wore a uniform. I suggested the president's house, which was across the street, and he agreed. He was driving the four hours from Bismarck and would arrive in about forty-five minutes.

I was about to give a special tour of the Stevens Hall renovation to Representative Sukut and Senator Lyson. I immediately emailed them to say that I would not be available. As I was leaving the college, I ran into Senator Lyson. I let him know a process server was coming to deliver a letter and I had to cancel the tour. He grinned. He also had experience with process servers. I laughed saying: "We are in Williston. You never know what will happen next." He wished me luck, and I rushed off home.

Waiting at home, I looked at my watch. I had another twenty minutes until the process server would arrive. It seemed like an eternity. My mind drifted to possible causes. The college's cash balances? Something related to the capital projects? The college's finances?

I created an entire list of possible reasons for why, in a matter of moments, the university system was going to take my keys and computer. The list was long, but I was not terribly worried. Nothing on the list had any legs.

On the other hand, the sheer number of items on the list could be the reason itself. I had taken on way too much risk at the college. I could see, given the number of risks taken cumulatively, why a process server was about to visit me.

The process server did not drive up in a patrol car as I anticipated. Instead, he drove his own car, was casually dressed, extremely pleasant and uncomfortably apologetic. The roles had become reversed. I was trying to put him at ease, which only added to his discomfort. He handed me the letter:

> Dear Dr. Nadolny,
>
> Subject: Paid Administrative Leave
>
> Effective immediately, I am placing you on paid administrative leave for an indefinite period.
>
> Unless escorted by me or my designee, you may not visit the Williston State College campus while on administrative leave. In addition, you may not contact WSC faculty or employees unless you have received permission from me or my designee.

You shall immediately return any property owned by Williston State College, including:

- Keys (both digital and physical)
- Vehicles
- Computers
- Documents (in digital and paper format)
- NDUS and WSC identification cards and badges

I am terminating your access to NDUS email, network, and digital files.

I am appointing an acting president to provide leadership to WSC during the period you are on administrative leave.

This action has been triggered by allegations of misconduct, where were brought to my attention earlier today. Accordingly, I will contract with an independent investigator to conduct a thorough investigation of the allegations. If the investigator concludes there is evidence to support the allegations, I will likely initiate action to dismiss you in accordance with paragraph 7 or 8 of SBHE Policy 305.1.

Sincerely,
Larry C. Skogen, Ph.D.
Interim Chancellor

"Allegations of misconduct?" I had served WSC for six years, spearheading a transformation of the College through unprecedented growth and challenges in the community. My performance reviews, year after year, had been exemplary. What type of allegations reported that very morning could draw this reaction from Larry only seven hours later?

The letter was ominous, suggesting I committed a crime. My job and my reputation were being damaged without detailing or naming the allegation. I was completely shocked, but I kept the emotion to myself. I did not want the process server to become more unsettled than he already was. After all, I was living in Williston. "Unsettled" had become a way of life.

I calmly handed over my keys and computer. I thanked him for bringing me the letter. He apologized again wishing me the best. It was now my turn to feel uncomfortable.

I immediately called Larry. He was already on the road to Williston. He asked to meet somewhere outside of campus. I asked if he remembered any places in Williston where he might feel comfortable. He remembered Pita Palace, a hole in the wall fast food restaurant across the street from the old community center. I agreed to meet him at 5 p.m. We would go over the situation then.

A few hours remained before my visit with the Interim Chancellor. I called Joyce and informed her of the letter. She was both compassionate and outraged. It was almost as if my wife had returned, providing me with the necessary moral courage. As the story would quickly make the papers, Joyce told me she would call and let my mom and dad know. I was incredibly grateful but thoroughly humiliated. From the sound of Joyce's voice on the phone, she was a rock of support, expressing confidence and even indignant anger on my behalf. At maybe during the most critical moment in my life, she was fully present and 100% behind me.

Just after 2:00 p.m., before I had the opportunity to meet with Larry, an all-campus email came out from the college's vice president of academic affairs: "Chancellor Skogen has put Dr. Raymond Nadolny on administrative leave effective immediately. And, the Chancellor has appointed the vice president for academic affairs as acting Interim President for Williston State College effective immediately. The Chancellor will hold a campus meeting for all personnel tomorrow morning – Thursday, October 16th – at 8:30 a.m. in Room 112 in the CTE Building." The vice president had jumped the gun and had sent out the email too early, an hour before I was to meet with the chancellor.

Meeting with the Chancellor

Pita Palace was on a busy street, so the meeting was anything but private. I met Larry outside, and we walked in together and found a seat in a booth behind large glass windows. He greeted me coolly.

Larry started. I had been placed on leave and requested to participate in a university system investigation regarding an event that took place a week earlier. The investigation was triggered by a claim that, if true, constituted "misconduct involving alcohol" at a campus event.

I had to search my mind for events a week prior. Recalling the night, I became surprised. Alcohol and misconduct? There had to be a mistake. When I attempted to speak to Larry about the evening, he would not listen. Judgment had been passed. He had come prepared to play hardball.

Around midnight of the day in question, I had just driven two hours to Minot to pick up the CEO from our Japanese sister college and then the two hours back to Williston. I slept a few hours and then was up again at 5:00 a.m. to start my work day which continued until 5:00 pm. Between 5:00 p.m. to 8:00 p.m., I hosted a welcome dinner at my home for the CEO. The evening of the event, my guest was jet lagged, so the festivities were decidedly low-key. In addition to the CEO, four staff members joined us for a rib dinner. We toasted the CEO with an alcoholic beverage from Japan called soju. The bottle of soju was a little smaller than a bottle of wine, and six people shared it.

After dinner, the CEO and I walked across the street to the college to attend a Halloween-themed student event called The Ghost Hunter which started at 8:00 p.m. The claim of "misconduct" involved this block of time. I had fallen asleep during the presentation.

I was now getting upset. Larry's letter was punitive, and the off-campus meeting was meant to intimidate. I was tired and was making a considerable effort to control my anger. He asked whether alcohol might be an issue for me.

I had already been judged and found guilty. Maybe I should have reacted? Like all things Williston, I took a step back. I tried to keep an open mind. I recalled being incredibly fatigued. I admitted to dozing off in the back of the room for a short while. I agreed that any appearance of not being fully present for a college event was inappropriate. I apologized for the distraction it had brought to the college, especially as the college and community were already in a stressful situation.

Larry was mollified. He then asked for me to do a substance abuse evaluation. I worked hard for the college, even subordinating my family for the good of the school and community. Within my sense of personal responsibility, I agreed to see a substance abuse evaluator. The whole time I was trying to temper the anger I was feeling at yet another injustice perpetrated by a system more eager to protect its image than the people in its care.

Even in my state of shock, I was still thinking about the college. I asked Larry to briefly reconsider his appointment of the Williston State's interim president. Before I could explain, he cut me off. For the time being, I was to have nothing to do with WSC. I was on a "short leash."

Larry requested I communicate with him only by phone. He reminded me that both email and texts were subject to public information requests. He asked me to call him the next day, and he would provide the name of a substance abuse counselor. With that, the meeting concluded.

By 7:25 p.m. that night, Larry emailed the other presidents an article on the incident from the *Williston Herald*. Again, the article was vague: "Interim Chancellor Larry Skogen confirmed the action, and said Nadolny's leave is due to alleged misconduct involving alcohol use." My already damaged reputation was now on its way to social media ruination. I was quickly becoming a one-man college reality show.

Later that night, it occurred to me why the rush to judgment had taken place. The State Board was on the eve of a vote on a constitutional measure to replace the State Board. The State Board was at risk. The university system was acting strongly and wanted to demonstrate that it would not be involved in a cover-up for one of its presidents—even if there was nothing to cover up. Larry reacted to the vote and not the situation. By taking such a draconian action, he was making a statement to protect the university system from the impending vote to eliminate the state board.

The university system went too far. By taking the very public and headline-making action of removing me physically, stripping me of my title, taking my keys, prohibiting entry to the college, confiscating my computer and files and my personal belongings at the college, depriving me of my community of friends and colleagues, and denying them access to me during this time of crisis, I was being defamed by false implication. I was not alcohol-impaired that night. No one drove a car that evening. But ultimately, there was nothing I could do when confronted seven days after the event.

Later, Larry would describe his actions as "harsh." He explained that he was "operating in an environment of hypersensitivity created by microscopic scrutiny since the governing State Board of Higher Education had fired my processor." The damage was done. My reputation was permanently damaged.

I understood what the university system was doing. It was protecting itself before a vote that would decide its very existence. I had a decision to make.

—

THE DAY AFTER

The problem with an untruth is that even if the lie gets disproved later, it always persists at some level. In this case, people misguidedly assumed due diligence had taken place before putting me on leave. I was very concerned this could quickly degenerate into a witch-hunt.

The decision was simple. I would tender my resignation. I entered higher education out of a sense of service. At this point, outside of a defamation lawsuit against the university system, which would serve no one, my service had come to an end. I would exit with a tarnished reputation. But I would exit on my terms and with what little dignity I could muster.

I set up the appointment with the substance abuse counselor and would communicate the results with the university system. I would then tender my resignation. I set up a time to meet with Larry the following Monday.

While I simmered over a situation that felt increasingly tragic, the Interim Chancellor was encountering difficulties of his own. He met in the morning with faculty and staff, then the executive cabinet. Staff did not understand fully what had happened and why I had been removed. Many were very concerned about Larry's appointing the vice president of instruction as my interim replacement.

There were several people who were with me on the night in question. As a result of Larry's letter, I was not allowed to contact them. Two members of executive cabinet shared with the chancellor that they had attended the dinner. They did not believe I was intoxicated.

On Friday, I called Larry and let him know I was going to resign. In a dramatic turnaround, Larry told me to be patient and that he might have made a mistake in appointing the interim president. He asked if we could meet in Bismarck on Monday and discuss what to do further. I let him know that my substance abuse evaluation was on Monday in Bismarck. I would meet with him afterward.

That evening alone in the townhouse in Bismarck, I unexpectedly heard children's chatter. I thought maybe I had drifted off to sleep and was dreaming. But then I heard the unmistakable sound of children's feet bounding up the stairs, and the two younger girls ran into my room, followed by Joyce shortly behind them. Joyce was worried about me and angered by what had transpired. She had flown out from Seattle on the first flight she could book and wanted to surprise me. I took Joyce into my arms and began to cry. She told me everything would be okay.

Joyce wanted me to hire a lawyer immediately and start legal action against the university system, but I shared with her my intention to resign. Although she did not fully understand my reasoning, she still supported me. Although the circumstances were horrible, it appeared the closer I came to losing my job, the closer I came to being with my family.

Substance Abuse Evaluation

I was fully committed to resigning and had the letter with me. It discussed my time at Williston State as one of the most challenging, yet most rewarding experiences in my life. I thanked the university system for the opportunity to serve such an outstanding institution and community. My resignation would take place immediately.

Unlike so many before me, I was not going to bargain for a buyout. I accepted my current position because I wanted to serve. Service no longer appeared to be an option. And given the impending vote to abolish the State Board, I certainly did not want to be named as the reason for its demise.

When I met Larry in his office, I placed the letter on his desk and pushed it toward him. He immediately pushed it back at me. Once again, he asked me to be patient.

There would be no investigation of the alleged alcohol violation. He reminded me how far the college had come over my tenure. I then let him know the results of my meeting with the substance abuse counselor. As I was a public figure, the recommendation was that I visit with a counselor to learn about alcohol abuse. I told the evaluator I would do so.

Larry did not look relieved. The vote on abolishing the State Board was on November 4, 2014, just over two weeks away. The university system had made a mistake but would be accused of a cover-up and of "protecting a president" if I was reinstated.

Larry told me I needed to take a break. I immediately knew where he was going. He suggested I take four weeks off to recover from my work in Williston. I was exhausted from playing games. I had grown weary over the constant neglect by the university system. I offered my resignation again.

I did not want to bring more burden and distraction to an already overtaxed college. It was not fair to add to the frustrations of my family. I told him to read the letter, as it was positive to both the college and the university system. Larry continued to push it back to me.

He said he needed me to take the time off. What he was really was saying was that he needed to get through the election with as little controversy as possible. He also confessed that he might have made a mistake on his appointment of the interim president. He needed my help and reasoned that if I took the break, I could return to work refreshed.

I reluctantly consented... with conditions. I wanted my computer back. He agreed. I wanted a specific date for my return. The college had to know with certainty that this nightmare had an end. We decided on November 19 as the date of my return, a day well past the vote on Measure 3.

We discussed the college assessment and agreed it would only create an additional burden on already overwhelmed employees. He promised it would only be a general review of the college and it would include no names. He had publically committed to the assessment, and he needed to keep his word.

He also needed to appoint a new interim president. Did I have a recommendation? "Terry Olson," I replied, "the Executive Director of the Foundation." He agreed immediately. He would call him that very day.

Before I left, he asked where I was going to stay over the next four weeks. I told him Williston. He asked if I could stay in my townhouse in Bismarck during my time off. I said no, much to his disappointment. My two step-daughters were still living with me in Williston. Bismarck was not an option.

Walking away from the meeting, it felt like I had fallen on my sword. I was now taking time off to regain my "health." There would be no clarification on the incident. To do so, would only create more controversy so close to the election. What had I gotten myself into... again?

That night, Larry sent out an email to the college presidents: "I've met a number of times with Dr. Nadolny. Everything from those meetings tells me that he'll return to his presidential responsibilities as noted in the statement. At your next Board meeting, I will be asking for your ratification of the appointment of Terry Olson as interim president."

The university system released a press release the next day:

> "Dr. Raymond Nadolny, president of Williston State College, has completed a medical evaluation and will be on leave from his position until approximately November 19. During this time, he will take advantage of health services that have been recommended by his healthcare provider. Dr. Nadolny's well-being and the well-being of Williston State College are our highest priorities, and I believe that these priorities are being served through this decision. It is no secret that there are unique challenges to all organizations currently operating in western North Dakota, and colleges are no different... I have full confidence in Dr. Nadolny and expect him to return to his position as president of WSC on or about Nov. 19."

A day after the press release, Joyce, I and the girls returned to our home in Williston. Joyce understood my decision to remain. But she had to get the younger girls back to Seattle as they could not miss more school. Joyce loved me. But Williston was no longer her home.

Looking out the window at the college, I felt like a man in prison. I could no longer trust that the Interim Chancellor would keep his word and that I would return as president on November 19. The process server, the confiscation of personal and professional materials, the sense of betrayal by a state and community I had poured my soul into at the expense of my family, and the enormous shadow this placed over the past five years were all devastating. On the other hand, compassion came from some unexpected places like the return of my family, a kind note from the governor's chief of staff, and a message of support from a blog writer unpopular with the university system presidents.

That afternoon, Terry and the lieutenant governor held a previously scheduled press conference to announce the Williams County Scholarship publicly. The announcement was to have been the most important moments of my career. I would read about it online.

—

THE RETURN

On November 4, the ballot measure to eliminate the State Board was soundly defeated. With the defeat of the ballot measure, the university system could once again take care of its own business. University employees Chief Auditor Timothy Carlson and Compliance Officer Kirsten Franzen were placed on notice. Carlson left quietly. Franzen, one of two attorneys hired by Chancellor Shirvani, would not leave without a fight. The university system's second attorney would eventually exit on her own.

Over the course of my prolonged "time-out" in Williston, paranoia struck again. The threat of Measure 3 was over. Two members of the university system staff were unceremoniously let go. I began to fear I would be the next employee terminated by the university system. Each day, I waited for another call from a process server. November 19 could not come soon enough.

When November 19, 2014, arrived, I nervously made my return to the campus. I was warmly welcomed. I sent an all-campus email apology for the disruption in leadership. The university system did not issue a press release. There was no story printed on my return. I relied on gossip to tell the real story.

The Trombley Report

"The purpose of the assessment was to gather information regarding the functioning of Williston State College's leadership in general... Several interviewees noted the positive aspects of Dr. Nadolny's visionary leadership, though not all agree with the direction he wishes to take the college. Even so, the sense one gets from speaking with the interviewees is that over all, he has been a positive force on the campus and is generally liked and appreciated."

—*Trombley Report*, November 2014

Right before Thanksgiving, Larry emailed me the *Trombley Report*, the assessment taken during my time-out from the college. A short time later, he called me. He agreed that there was nothing in the report we did not already know.

Larry had told both my staff and me that those interviewed would not be identified by name in the report. The report listed the names of the staff members interviewed. I reminded him of that promise to both staff and myself that the names would not be included in the report. He became short tempered. As far as he was concerned, the matter was over, and I could use the report as I liked.

I shared the report with the Director of Human Resources. I wanted to get her take on the report before I shared it with Executive Cabinet. She became upset. Interviewees were listed in the document, so it was relatively easy to attribute comments to specific staff members.

One negative comment aimed at the HR Director caused her significant grief. I could empathize, of course. I was an administrator with over 25 years of experience. Listening to critical feedback, often aimed at me directly, was a part of the job. But I had developed a thick skin, whereas most members of the executive cabinet had less than three years of experience and were not used to criticism, especially public criticism.

I waited until staff returned from Thanksgiving Break. I would let them know I had received the report. Unless the college received a public information request, which was likely, I would not distribute it.

I told executive cabinet that the names of the people interviewed were included in the report, which angered some. They felt personally betrayed by the interim chancellor. I informed executive cabinet of my conversation with Larry as well as his comments that the matter was now over. There was nothing more to be done; we had to move forward.

If any cabinet member wanted a copy, I would provide it to them. But as the staff was given a promise before the interviews that their names would not appear in the report, and that promise was broken, everyone agreed that it would be best to shelve the report. No one from cabinet requested a copy. Surprisingly, no one from the press or the legislature filed a public information request for it either. The report, like my reputation, was buried.

Chapter 12
BUST

TRANSFORMATION

The boom occurred over an incredible stretch of five-plus years. The bust would be much faster. Still devastated by being unceremoniously removed from office, I was on the other hand delirious with the knowledge that the college had survived the boom. Not only had we survived the boom, we had set up a solid infrastructure to weather the bust.

After five years of chaos, Williston State resumed normal operations. The renovation of Stevens Hall was completed two weeks ahead of schedule. I was back in my office. All accounted, the college's extreme makeover included a new residence hall, a new technical building, a new front and back drive, a renovated academic building, new streets, a new science wing and a workforce training building still under construction.

Indeed, on the opening day of Spring 2014, Williston State's enrollment increased 13.24%. The increase was remarkable given that the Williams County Scholarship would not begin until the following fall. Enrollment projections for Fall were off the chart (+60%). The opening of Stevens Hall and the increase in enrollment could not have happened at a better time.

Now, with the legislature in session, all I had to do was show my face, pretend nothing happened, and hope the Legislature would allow the college to retain the two million dollars in operational funding awarded in the last session.

Falling

> In neighboring Watford City, Mayor Brent Sanford used a personal example to illustrate the growth: When his daughter was born in 2000, there were three other babies born in the county that year. Now there are 90 kids in her class. 'Half the students are living in RVs,' said Sanford, speaking to the acute shortage of housing that still plagues the area. 'It's inhumane.'"
>
> —CNN, January 22. 2015[57]

Workers, once coming in droves to the oil patch, were now beginning to leave. Many oil patch employees had regularly padded their salaries with exorbitant amounts of overtime, but now overtime was getting cut as company budgets were getting downsized, and easy and plentiful sources of income were quickly drying up.

Oil prices continued to act in a way that allowed conservatives to say, "We have no money," and liberals to say, "We are in a good position." So the environment was still highly reactionary to the price of oil. What a change from five years earlier, when people would regularly downplay the impact of oil on the state's economy.

The university system was still trying to hold on to the diminishing optimism surrounding a turnaround in oil prices. *Bloomberg* was reporting a quicker than expected recovery in oil, and the direct beneficiaries, according to its reporters would be shale oil producers. Oil prices were now driving most of the conversation and legislative actions in the Capitol.

Once again, the college provided testimony to the House appropriations committee. Two state board members attended. Larry stepped in sporadically. I acknowledged to the Committee that the two million dollars awarded in the last session created variables within the funding model. At the same time, the funding allowed the college to stabilize its wages. Although turnover was slowing, the college was still grappling with inexperienced workers crippling its ability to assume normal operations.

The Committee Chair, Representative Monson, pulled me aside after the presentation. A farmer and a retired school administrator, Representative Monson was also a graduate of UND-Williston. He was surprised at the candor of my testimony. He wondered if the university system really understood Williston State's situation. I said yes. Most people, when confronted with the full picture, could not believe that that the university system had taken no action. But, as I was the president who was mysteriously whisked from office, maybe, people thought, I wasn't giving them the full story.

Still, my testimony met with a positive response. In January of 2015, legislators kept a lingering hope in the back of their minds that oil would make a comeback. So, the college and northwest North Dakota, to a certain degree, had the ear of the legislature. This privilege would change quickly. Outside of my presentation, committee members were already talking about cutting higher education.

A day after my testimony, Standard and Poor's downgraded the college's residence hall rating to junk bond status. With the loss of revenue from Dickson Hall and the loss of almost $30,000 from the federal governments sequester, the college no longer received the necessary cash flow from housing. Student housing fees would have to increase significantly.

Once again, I was attending committee meetings trying to keep legislators informed of the college's situation. Larry, like Chancellor Shirvani, would not allow Laura, the Vice Chancellor of Finance to attend the legislative committee meetings. And again, Laura was using my notes to send updates to the colleges' business officers to keep them updated on the university sytem's progress with the legislature.

Conversations out of the House higher education committee were now far more concerning than those from the last session. A dip in the economy was providing an opportunity to wield an ax at higher education. And there was still a lot of lingering resentment left over from legislator's conflict with Chancellor Shirvani.

The college was also on the House's chopping block. With Representative Skarphol now removed from the inner circle and an opportunity to correct the performance funding model, the House Higher Education Appropriations Committee removed $2.5 million from the college's base. The State Board paid no attention to the House pulling $2.5 million from Williston State's base. People in the western part of the state were much more vocal, and members of the committee received significant public pressure to place the funding back. The House would eventually relent, but it took an incredible final push by the community.

State Board Update

"Finally, all but three colleges saw an addition to their base funding. Williston State was one of the exceptions with a cut of almost $400,000. Given my communication about Williston's cash flow with OMB, the University System and State Board this past summer; given Williston State's residence hall bond rating moving to junk status; given Williston State's audit issues related to turnover reported both to the State Board and the various legislative committees; given Williston State now having to bring forward a 40% increase in residence hall rates just to break even in the current environment; I am truly perplexed at what additional evidence is required to demonstrate that the state's fastest growing college in the country's highest cost region is in need of support, not a decrease in resources much less conversations about closing higher education access to degree seeking students."

—2015 February Williston State Presentation to State Board

As the community went from boom to bust, new challenges emerged for the college. Williston State had a $2.5 million loan from the Bank of North Dakota for a workforce facility that would not open for months. With the downturn in oil prices and Williston State's lack of cash flow, the college was concerned with TrainND's decreasing revenue. One of the first things struggling businesses cut was training. The building was not even completed, and the college was worried about making the bank payments.

Housing, athletics, the cafeteria and the bookstore were posting huge losses. Each auxiliary program had to operate solely on the income they received. How were government-run programs to survive when Walmart increased starting wages from $15 per hour to $17 per hour for unskilled labor?

The finance office proposed significant increases in fees and student housing. Because of the new recreation center, the finance office was also asking for a dramatic increase in the recreation fee. Inflation was taking a financial toll on students. Fortunately, the foundation's generous scholarship absorbed much, if not all the cost.

The university system itself was once again in panic mode. A legislative ax was about to fall yet again on the State Board. At the State Board's May meeting, the college's fee increases passed with little conversation as the Board was preoccupied with its own budget concerns. Williston State would later pay a heavy price for the Board's lack of involvement.

Cry for Help

After quadrupling its debt in the past four years, the municipality (Williston) finds itself a victim of its own success just as the energy juggernaut shows signs of slowing. Its leaders are bracing for a slowdown with oil prices down about 53 percent since June, to about $49 a barrel. Williston still needs to provide for its citizens. It's behind in offering adequate housing and maintaining roads, sewers and water systems to accommodate energy workers. The region's infrastructure has crumbled even as the state reaped $6 billion in oil and natural-gas tax revenue from fiscal 2006 through January, according to the Legislative Council.

—Bloomberg, February 1, 2015[58]

Representative Skarphol fell off everyone's radar. He kept to himself, occasionally dropping into his assigned committees. Despite his diminished influence, no one could understand the impact Representative Skarphol had made to both the college and the community during the boom. He was still the college's last hope and needed to be lured back into circulation to help us with the bust.

After some serious searching, I finally tracked him down and persisted until he sat down with me for coffee. His first response was that I should not be seen with him. He was "persona non-grata" at the legislature and warned me that association by appearance would only damage any request I was making.

Skarphol made it clear that he had become a pariah in the legislature. I asked whether he ever thought of falling on his sword for the region and groveling before Representative Carlson. With a sneer, he said that would never happen.

Before the session started, Skarphol was called in to meet with Carlson, who was handing out committee assignments. Carlson was sitting behind a desk, Representative Delzer, a farmer and chair of appropriations, was sitting next to him. Carlson asked Skarphol what committee he wanted to serve on. Skarphol told him appropriations (the most powerful committee). Carlson tried to steer him elsewhere, to which Skarphol responded that if he were not placed on appropriations, he would not attend any committee meetings. And with that line drawn in the sand, Skarphol effectively severed his relationship with the inner circle. The once powerful advocate for northwest North Dakota was done.

By April of 2015, the overall belief among the legislators was that inflation was no longer a factor in the western part of the state. Legislators believed that the college's enrollment increases would result in additional funding for the college. The conference committee rejected placing $2.5 million back into Williston State's base. They did, however, move two million dollars to one-time funding. The college was safe for at least another biennium.

On the last day of conference committee meetings, I overheard Carlson saying to Holmberg: "Do you want the good news or the bad news?" Holmberg quickly responded: "Well, you're here. What is the good news?" Representative Carlson and Senator Holmberg continued to make deals and divvy up the budget. The absence of Representative Skarphol was painfully felt. For the first time in six years, a share of the budget would not be returning to northwest North Dakota.

Some things, as one legislative conference committee member told me, needs to be taken on faith. Sometimes, the most we can expect is that our concern is acknowledged and understood despite the outcome. Oil prices were spiraling. And with a series of negative state revenue projections and budget forecasts, faith seemed a lot to ask.

Clinging to Hope

"When one boy among a dozen throws a stone into the air, crying out, that 'what goes up must come down,' it is very likely so to happen."
—Theodore Sedgwick's *Hints to my Countrymen*, 1826

Larry continued to express optimism about a return to more robust oil prices. His sentiment did not resonate in Williston. Companies were digging in for a prolonged oil draught.

When oil was king, everyone jumped on board. Now the ride was over. Larry was grasping at any positive sign as the university system office was also subjected to massive cuts. For the first time in six years, the university systems office would go through greater turnover than Williston State.

The college had much to be grateful. The college had weathered the boom. The college had not only survived but played a vital role in the life of the community. Sure, Williston State would have to be smart on the use of the one-time dollars. But the college was more confident in its ability to survive a bust. And for the first time in ten years, the college had the beginning of a reserve.

—

DOWNSIZED

"Oil prices have fallen by over half since last summer. In oil producing states like North Dakota, that's caused widespread layoffs and a huge slowdown in oilfield activity. But one thing hasn't changed – rents. In and around the Bakken oil field, they are among the highest in the nation."

—Inside Energy, April 3, 2015[59]

Because of the legislative session, the university system was downsized significantly. The Chief of Staff, Murray Sagsveen was stepping down. Sitting in the Capitol building over lunch, Murray confessed to me that his biggest regret during his time with the university system was the handling of my removal in the fall. He apologized. It was the first time anyone from the university system expressed any remorse or anything close to an apology. The entire episode was painful. It had likely cost me any future career as a president, but I was still grateful for the words.

Larry could not wait to return to his former position as President of Bismarck State College. He was a favored son of Bismarck. But in his 18-month tenure as interim chancellor, he weathered an accreditation visit and a referendum vote only to be beaten up by legislators on a regular basis over the course of the legislative session. A permanent chancellor would now come on board.

At the State Board's April 30, 2015, meeting, Mark Hagerott was selected as the university system's new chancellor. It was difficult to believe things would change, but Hagerott certainly said the right things. Maybe third time was a charm. I had hope.

Family life was still a disaster. Joyce made the unilateral decision to leave and head back to Seattle where she would spend a year living in a 300 square foot apartment, making only marginal inroads into restarting her career as she struggled as a single mother of two young daughters and became separated from her two older daughters who asked to remain in Williston.

Meanwhile, I managed to successfully care for my two step-daughters. Kiana, a junior, was graduating from high school a year early and Sophia was enjoying her freshman year. Without mom in Williston, I was in charge of Kiana's attending prom.

Several of Kiana's friends and some of their family would take pictures at my house before prom. Kiana was fine, but I was a nervous wreck. When Kiana's dress broke, I was reminded once again that my situation was both comic and tragic. As some parents of the prom couples had come to the President's House to take pictures, I was able to recruit a mother to assist Kiana. I prayed the situation would be resolved without any involvement from me. The dress was repaired, photos were taken and prom night was a success. Like everything else in Williston and in life, you just have to take the wins with the losses.

By the end of that school year, Joyce agreed to have the little girls come back to Williston. In the fall of 2015, Julia and Emma would be returning to Williston Public School's first and third-grade classes. Kiana would start her first semester as a freshman at the University of Washington. Sophia was getting ready for her sophomore year of high school in Williston. The house in Williston would once again be filled with the constant chatter of the girls. The only one missing would be Joyce.

Chapter 13
COMPROMISED

"It's no secret that you have had your challenges at your institution. These challenges were compounded this legislative session when you lost base funding. We both know that it's difficult to plan a road-ahead, particularly regarding your staffing issues, when you're dealing with one-time funding. But I also know that you've been under terrible pressures in the past, and you've pulled through. Your institution is better for it. Finally, I long for a system office having the resources that could help alleviate dome of your shortfall. As you've heard me say before, I wished I had a SWAT team that I could send into an institution to work on major issues. But I don't. So left to your own resources, you've done an amazing job of working through a plethora of problems, big and small. Thank you for that."

AN OFFICER AND MAYBE NOT A GENTLEMAN

Mark Hagerott was the Former Deputy Director and Distinguished Professor of Cyber Operations and Policy at the Center for Cyber Studies at the U.S. Naval Academy. Hagerott served in the Navy as a nuclear engineer and ship commander. A graduate of the United States Naval Academy, he held an MA in economics and a Ph.D. in Science and Technology Studies from the University of Maryland.

Hagerott was originally from North Dakota: "My background is fourth-generation family farm in North Dakota. My great-grandfather settled there, and it's something I hold dear," Hagerott stated. "My dad, at 80 years of age, is still farming, and I come back from time to time to help him out."

Hagerott quickly distanced himself from Shirvani whose tenure was marked by an autocratic style. The colleges breathed a collective sigh of relief when the newly appointed chancellor stated: "Communication flow and transparency will enhance the collaboration between the universities and stakeholders."

Hagerott formally began his job on July 1, 2015, with a salary set at $372,000 per year. Like Shirvani, his contract was meant to place him at a level above the presidents. It was unclear whether the State Board was taking a step forward or a step back. Once again, confusion set in and university presidents began to wonder if they were reporting to the State Board or the chancellor.

Hagerott's contract should have been a warning sign. The State Board was slowly returning to the autocratic style used by Shirvani. But unlike Shirvani's in-your-face approach, Hagerott ruled with a smile. With each chancellor, and there were four in my seven years, my expectations had only increased. This was especially unfair to the chancellors as the State Board kept filling the position with out of state candidates. Coming from out of state myself and with six years under my belt, who would know better the difficulty of working and living in both the university system and North Dakota? But as college rode the boom and the bust, abandoned by the system, I only became more frustrated. Terry would smile and tell me to relax. And even knowing the system was broke, rightly or wrongly, I just couldn't help feeling that the State Board and the chancellor owed the college so much more.

Limited university system support continued to come from Laura Glatt, the vice chancellor for finance. Laura was the saving grace of the university system. Laura served as a university system shield to unhospitable legislators, whom, under the last three chancellors, pushed for her termination. The legislators would finally get their way as the vice chancellor would soon resign, taking a position in the Colorado University System. The college lost its final advocate in the university system office.

On Sept 24, 2015 record final numbers for fall enrollment were released. Even with the closing of the college's Minot nursing program and the downsizing of two other programs, full-time students increased by 43%, and freshmen increased by 26%. More incredibly, the number of classes being taken increased 28%.

Recovery

Even with the economic slowdown, the college began to make remarkable progress in all divisions. Turnover slowed. Employees were gradually gaining more and more experience. For the first time in years, the Finance Office was fully staffed. At least for the college, the bust was turning out to be a well needed break.

I moved out of my new office in Stevens Hall into the last spot on campus still not renovated so that instruction could have an entire suite of offices. Given the State's current budget deficit, I decided to do a less than extreme makeover on my office, my assistant's office, and the remaining music faculty member's office. On the weekends, I painted the offices and replaced the tiles in my ceiling. After five years of the boom, I was secretly enjoying the Bust.

It was while I was painting my office when a student stopped by to speak to me about a tax problem. Between financial aid and the foundation scholarship, he was going to be paying taxes. A lot of taxes. It occurred to me that the foundation scholarship could be stretched even further. I suggested to Terry that financial aid should be applied before the foundation's scholarship kicked in. He agreed. As a result, the scholarship would break new ground eventually reaching into the state of Montana.

Life was returning to normal at the college and I was recovering nicely from my brief expulsion. But as the university system was knee deep in yet another leadership transition, the college would not remain off the university system's radar for long.

—

SET UP

I received an email requesting time to meet with Eric Killelea, the *Williston Herald*'s oil and energy reporter. He wanted to meet about the tuition and fee increases approved by the State Board almost three months earlier (an old story by journalist standards). He brought the minutes from the May State Board meeting, but not the agenda, which provided the detailed rationale for the college's proposed tuition and fee changes. I let the reporter know that the agenda was on the same web page as where he had found the minutes at which point the meeting ended.

On August 12, almost three months after the State Board approved raising fees at Williston State, the *Williston Herald* published their story: "Room and Fees go Boom at WSC." Natalie and Jennie from the marketing department were incensed and wanted to respond. I told them to wait. They needed to see if the story spiraled. In the meantime, I instructed them to fact check the story.

The article had nine significant errors and numerous minor errors, which we provided to both the university system and the publisher of the *Herald*. The *Herald* published an online retraction, but the damage was done. Three days after publication of the original article, other news agencies had picked up the story. The story had now spiraled.

The chief of staff called me to let me know that Hagerott would be placing the State Board's earlier approval of the college's tuition and fees back on the State Board agenda. As most business is done face to face in North Dakota, I requested permission from Hagerott to personally visit with key legislators like Senator Holmberg as well as various State Board members. I even suggested that I take Senator Bekkedahl with me.

Hagerott instructed me to take a step back. He would take care of it. Hagerott had all the information at his fingertips. The process was followed per the State Board rules and previously approved by the State Board. He asked me to trust him. Once again, I had been asked to trust a university system that time and again had let both the college and me down.

I felt guilty about the possibility of going behind the chancellor's back. I spoke with Terry who again suggested that I "drink the Kool-Aid." The chancellor was new. It was possible I was overreacting to five plus years of university system alternating neglect and interference. I drank more Kool-Aid.

Deceived

Williston State has tried to keep its costs down and at one point did not raise tuition for five years, Nadolny told the board. The college in 2013 had $30,000 in its bank account and a payroll of $250,000, he said, and has worked its way to becoming fiscally solvent. Morton told The Associated Press after the meeting that it's tricky because Williston State, like other colleges, depends on bonding in order to keep the cost of borrowing down. "Otherwise it really gets expensive and the students end up paying that," he said. "There's a lot that goes into the whole fee structure that's very detailed and it's something that the public has a hard time digesting." Morton said Hagerott needs time to "analyze the situation, talk to all the right parties, and then come up with the solution that works for everyone."

—*Washington Times*, September 3, 2015[60]

Immediately before the State Board meeting, Hagerott again asked me not to speak about the fees. He said he did not want to open a can of worms. He would bring his people to review the fees and before I knew it, the whole thing would go away. Against my better judgment, I gave in to Hagerott's request. I handed out my presentation and only provided a light summary of the fees during my presentation. I was losing my taste for Kool-Aid quickly.

When I finished my presentation, the State Board remained silent. Not one question was asked. Given the media coverage, I started to feel more comfortable. Behind closed doors, maybe Hagerott had smoothed the way. Terry was right.

When the agenda item on fees came up, Hagerott did exactly what he said he would. The Chancellor expressed confidence in Williston State. The university system would "study" the situation. I felt comfortable and embarrassed. I was wrong. I overreacted. I had gone through too much in the university system. I had obviously become jaded. Maybe the Kool-Aid wasn't so bad after all.

Then it happened. At the very end of the meeting, Don Morton, the acting State Board chair, instead of closing the State Board meeting, read from a prepared statement. He announced that at the next board meeting, based on what was discovered in the Chancellor's study of Williston State fees, he would place a motion to both reduce Williston State fees in 2016-2017 and reimburse Williston State fees retroactively from 2015-2016. In other words, not only was he calling for a reduction in fees that supported services in a high inflation environment, he was asking that an already cash depleted college reimburse fees.

I had been set up. The newspapers went wild with the story based on Don's one-line statement. Williston State was headline news. The story was picked up across the nation. Don promptly closed the State Board meeting.

I immediately made a beeline for Don. I asked him what was going on; he had always been a supporter of the college. Why would he make such a statement without even talking to me first? Why were there no questions asked after my presentation?

He immediately became flustered. To my surprise, he even

looked embarrassed. He informed me that the State Board was fully behind the college. He was given the statement by the State Board office to read so the university system could appear responsive to Senator Holmberg. He once again assured me of the State Board's full support. Don had also been used.

I headed next for Hagerott. Once again, as was his manner, he said all the right things. He reinforced that the situation would be addressed through the study. I asked him directly why Don's statement, written in advance, had not been communicated to me. Hagerott pivoted.

He again assured me that the situation would be looked into and addressed. I reminded him about his communication over the past week. He pivoted again saying everything would be taken care of over time, and he just needed time.

I took a step back. I found myself once again in a system that worried more about itself then the college. It was not the time to go on the offensive. I needed to take a step back and regain my composure. I told Hagerott what I told our local legislators and Representative Sanford at the end of the last session. I would have faith in the university system. If my faith in the system would not be rewarded, then at the very least, I would have a story to tell about poisoned Kool-Aid.

System Office's Review of Fees

Less than a week after the State Board meeting, I spent two days with Laura Glatt, the Vice Chancellor of Finance and a team from the University of North Dakota. It was not a study as the chancellor promised. Laura arrived on campus with a directive to decrease Williston State's fees.

One week after Laura's review, Hagerott announced Laura's resignation as vice chancellor for finance. Laura sent me an email a day after the announcement: "I consider you among my greatest colleagues and friends. I have told others repeatedly, including Lisa (chief of staff) again this week, that I am amazed by your energy, commitment, understanding of and support of WSC.... under very challenging circumstances. You are truly an unsung hero." It was a nice note, but it was by no means comforting. The problem with heroes is that they are often killed.

—

LEGISLATIVE INTERFERENCE

The chancellor had already made the decision for us. We compromised on fees. The only question now was: what had we compromised? I arranged a phone call with Hagerott to find out.

At the scheduled time, my phone rang and I picked up. Hagerott said: "Ray, thank you for taking my call."

I was a little surprised since I was the one that set up the call, but before I could say anything, Hagerott started to talk about the UND presidential search. He was wondering if I had anyone I would recommend to be UND's interim president.

I was impressed. Maybe Hagerott was getting input from all the presidents on the selection of the UND interim president. No matter, it was a step in the right direction.

I said I had no recommendations, but I deeply appreciated that he sought my input. The Chancellor then brought up the college. He discussed Williston State like a third party. I began to doubt that he had the right person on the phone. He discussed a 50% percent reduction in fees. He wanted my input.

I then said: "Chancellor, you do know this is Ray Nadolny you are speaking with?" Momentary silence. Then he apologized. He had both myself and Senator Ray Holmberg on his calendar and mistakenly thought, when his secretary sent over the call, that he was speaking with Ray Holmberg. He confused our voices as Senator Holmberg was in Europe on vacation. He presumed it was a bad line.

I was incredulous. Hagerott was seeking direction from the Senate's highest ranking legislator on the interim president for UND. Hagerott was also briefing the Senator on Williston State's fees and looking for input before speaking with the college's president.

Hagerott handled the uncomfortable moment by laughing the phone call off. He continued with the conversation on fees. Yes, he would recommend a 50% reduction in the fees starting the spring, but the reduction would not be retroactive.

In that one phone call, everything was made clear. Colleges were not in charge. Legislators were now key to the university system decision-making process. Decisions were already being discussed with legislative leadership before consulting the college's president. I answered: "Okay."

The chancellor, the chief of staff, and the chair of the State Board would never place Williston State's 50% reduction in fees on the State Board's agenda. The changes to the fee structure would never even be reported to the State Board. To the surprise of the college's leadership, once the college reduced the fees, the matter vanished. My staff was angry. For myself, it had become business as usual in the university system. I could do nothing but grin, bear it, and hope the chancellor's focus would eventually shift somewhere else. But the process made it abundantly clear to me, my time with the university system was coming to an end.

Under Pressure

"North Dakota's oil boom has gone bust, leaving the state government with a gaping $1 billion hole in its two-year budget."

—CNN Money, February 2, 2016[61]

Once flooded with cash, North Dakota now found itself in economic chaos. In Williston, Halliburton shut down three fracking crews (about 300 employees). Whiting would most likely shut down their operations in Dickinson and consolidate in Watford City. Senator Bekkedahl he informed me that the city of Williston's bond rating was downgraded from A to BB. The college's bond rating for FY15 remained the same: BB. I took this as a victory.

Dawson Community College, 100 miles from Williston State, had been through three presidents in the last three years. The job profile in the Chronicle for Higher Education was telling: "Beginning in late 2012, the trustees took action resulting in a complete turnover in administrative leadership at the college. The new leaders of Dawson Community College were given a mandate to transform the operations of the college in an aggressive and comprehensive manner. Since that time, the college has undergone sweeping reforms and strategic repositioning. The next president will need a high risk tolerance and find satisfaction in new initiatives and accomplishments."[62] The position sounded exactly like my job.

When the state announced across the board budget cuts, I sat down to dinner and explained the situation to my daughters Emma (1st Grade), Julia (3rd Grade), and Sophia (Sophomore). I let them know that the Governor had asked the college to reduce budgets by 4.05% this year and 4.05% next year. They asked a lot of questions.

Julia said she wanted to help and was going to give $5. She asked where she should give the money. I thought for a moment and told her the Governor. So, Julia wrote a note to the Governor, took five dollars from her piggy bank, and put it in an envelope. I mailed it the next day.

Julia's gift, rather, the motive behind the gift told me Williston State would more than adequately deal with the budget reductions. At 4.05%, Williston State's cuts would not result in any jobs eliminated. The best way for Williston State to ensure student success, especially after years of turnover, was for Williston State to ensure the employees' success.

Dinner with the Chancellor

I requested a meeting with Hagerott to go over the college's finances. A meeting was set up through his secretary. I was asked to join Hagerott for dinner at a restaurant close to his home.

We were to dine at 7:30 p.m. at Seven Seas Restaurant. As I was driving to the dinner, Hagerott called me on my cell. He was dealing with movers. Could we meet at his home in Mandan? I said yes.

Hagerott then directed me to pick up a "burger without cheese" at a Burger King a couple blocks from his home. He would reimburse me when I arrived at his house. I should also get something for myself. I did as Hagerott requested.

I had been on the road for four hours. I was redirected from dinner at a restaurant to picking up fast food. I was pissed. Sitting at his dining room table, I unwrapped my cheeseburger and decided to go straight to my first question: "How could I help my finance office? They were feeling strapped by increasing demands from the university system." He told me to talk to the System's CFO.

I asked my second question: "While the college reduced fees, the State Board chose to ignore a 2780% fitness facility fee increase at Valley City University and the near doubling of two aquatic fees at NDSU and NDSC. Not one question by the State Board was asked. Why was there a double standard?" Hagerott called the matter political. I was getting nowhere.

After a long drive and a cheeseburger, I was growing impatient. I said: "University system enrollment was anemic: -0.57 for community colleges; -8.43% for regional colleges and; 1.51% for universities. Williston State's enrollment growth over the same time was +28%. Did the Board understand the dramatic changes taking place at the college?" Hagerott assured me the board understood our situation.

Hagerott was looking for an exit. He said he did not know the conversation would be quite this extensive. He would need some time and then we could revisit the conversation again.

As we parted at the door, I made a positive comment on his home. He shared with me that between his retirement and his current position, he was making over half a million dollars per year. Not really understanding the fast food dinner, the lack of meaningful conversation, or where that comment came from, I shut my mouth and left. No longer feeling effective, I had some serious decisions to make.

Chapter 14
RESIGNED

Williston State College President Dr. Raymond Nadolny announced his resignation to the faculty and staff Monday morning. Nadolny will maintain his position until the conclusion on his contract on June 30, 2017 which will provide ample time to begin the selection process for WSC fourth president. The difficult decision, he said, was rooted in his desire to be with family.

—The Williston Herald, May 17, 2016[63]

TRANSITION

The Sunday before graduation, I called Joyce. There was no answer. I called late into the night. She picked up the phone. I asked: "Were you out?" She replied: "Yes." I asked where and she gave me the name of a restaurant. I asked if she was with a girlfriend I knew she frequently visited with. She responded with a no. I asked her directly: "Who were you with?" She hesitated and then responded: "My friend...." I started running through a gamut of questions only to find myself increasingly humiliated in the process. I made my decision. I was resigning. It might be too late to save my marriage, but I was not going to have it end without some effort on my part.

The college was getting stronger and stronger. We had completed three master plans in seven years. My dealings with the university system now seemed more personal than professional. Maybe I was no longer the best person to represent the college. At graduation, the college would celebrate the unveiling of its third piece of artwork during my tenure. And Williston State was in its best health since I had become president seven years earlier. It was truly time to go, truth be told. I might soon be left with nothing, not even my family.

I would tender my resignation after graduation and salvage what I could of my marriage. Early morning on Saturday, May 15, the day after graduation, I stunned Joyce by texting her with my decision to resign on Monday morning.

The Governor's Unintended Consequences

While I was penning my resignation letter, the Governor's Office of Management and Budget released the 2017-19 Budget Guidelines. Williston State's budget would be reduced by almost a third. Part of me was getting sucked backed into the college, but there was one difference.

This time, even in a worst-case scenario, the college would be able to weather the state cuts for at least one biennium. The college had successfully accumulated almost $2.7 million in reserves. The downside was that it would most likely have to expend its entire reserves (an accreditation violation) if the state chose not to account for its most recent enrollment growth.

A day before graduation, an opportunity presented itself. The college was notified that Lieutenant Governor Drew Wrigley would be attending Williston State's graduation. I emailed Hagerott letting him know I planned to apprise the Lieutenant Governor of the 28% to 33% potential biennium cut to Williston State's base. The Governor's Office and I enjoyed a warm relationship. The Governor was intimately familiar with Williston State's unique situation as an oil impact college and the college needed the Governor's continued support.

Hagerott instructed me to speak with his chief of staff Lisa Feldner, so I called her. She was clear. Do not to speak with the Lieutenant Governor.

I asked Lisa if the system had a plan if Williston State was asked to present a proposal to cut one-third of its budget (a likely scenario given the Governor's initial guidance). She said the system had no plan. Williston State would have to wait until guidance was clear. A plan would then be put together.

I followed her directive. But for the first time in my position as president, I had lost faith in the university system. There would be no magic worked from Skarphol, no miracle last-second save. My multiple successful funding requests that created a ripple in the performance funding model now made me an ineffective agent of the college. My decision to resign was reconfirmed.

The Sunday after graduation, I sent my resignation letter to the Chancellor and copied the Chair of the State Board. I would complete the remaining 14-months on my contract. The Board Chair, Kathleen Neset, was surprised: "I am stunned by your resignation."

Most staff were not surprised. The *Williston Herald* reported what had become my mantra: "The difficult decision, he said, was rooted in his desire to be with family." And with my resignation, just like my earlier forced removal from the college, I was drawn immediately closer to both Joyce and my daughters.

Meeting with Chancellor

Just prior to a State Board retreat, Hagerott and I were discussing how the needs of northwest North Dakota could be addressed in his proposed Envision 2030 initiative. I let him know I had conducted a great deal of research on the matter. He made me a proposition.

If I were to change my resignation date, I could work for him between August and March putting together a paper that could be included in Envision 2030. I could even work from home and be with my family in Seattle. The offer was enticing.

I had recently learned that my father's chemotherapy was no longer working. And after being so immersed in Williston, I would have the opportunity to catch up on time lost with him. And there was no denying it. Pressure from the legislature was now a relentless force behind this latest chancellor.

I made my decision. My experience in Williston was everything I could hope for in a mission and not hope for in a mission. I had overcome both natural disasters and human-made disasters. I had survived floods, snow storms, ice storms, dust storms, and mosquito swarms. I had survived my college's relationship with a strip club, near bankruptcy, a sex offender on campus, public scandal, and four chancellors. I even averted a scandal with the great grandson of Sitting Bull.

Battling the latest chancellor would only be an exercise in futility. And with Skarphol gone, I used up any remaining chips I possessed. It was now time for the next generation of leadership to stand up for a community "that had settled for far too little, for far too long." It was time for me to return to my family.

I asked Hagerott if I could step down after my return from Japan at the end of June. It would provide an interim president two months to make sure the college was ready for the start of classes in the fall. I could then work for Hagerott on the paper identifying the challenges and opportunities in northwest higher education. He agreed. Hagerott was pleased, and I was relieved. A new president would now have their turn in the sun.

There was still one thing left to do. I reminded Hagerott that we still needed to complete my evaluation. He told me not to worry, that it would be very good. He would take care of everything. Not surprisingly, Hagerott never got around to it.

Special Board Meeting

"The North Dakota University System's renewed commitment to openness and transparency is welcome. We trust Chancellor Mark Hagerott when he said in an interview that the transformation is deliberate, and that the board is making an extra effort to comply with open-meetings laws...

Nothing was more damaging to the board during the "bad years" than the seeming willfulness with which it repeatedly broke open-meetings laws. And nothing will prove so rejuvenating to the public trust than the board's success at keeping this new compliance alive."

—*Grand Forks Herald*, September 6, 2016

At the end of June, I attended my last executive cabinet meeting at the college. That same day, Hagerott's assistant sent an email from the systems office announcing a special board meeting. The notice for the meeting was 15 minutes. The agenda items were approval of my resignation and approval of Williston State's interim president. By the time I read the email, the board meeting was already over, and I had missed it.

I emailed Hagerott the next day to find out the result of the State Board meeting. His response:

> "Yes. Agreement approved. Unanimous. And when i catch my breath will start process (president) emeritus. Just put that on your resume as proposed by chancellor, which i did say publically, and "now pending state board approval". Lets grab coffee sometime in Bismarck. Talk theology and Bakken."

Hagerott had also promised through various media outlets that he would nominate me for the honorary title of president emeritus. I was honored. The college's faculty, staff, and student senate presidents signed a resolution of support. But when the chancellor decided to take on the president of North Dakota State Univeristy, he asked me if he could delay bringing my nomination forward until the January, 2017, State Board meeting. I said of course. The nomination never went to the Board.

—

CONCLUSION

"You who live your lives in cities or among peaceful ways cannot always tell whether your friends are the kind who would go through fire for you. But on the Plains one's friends have an opportunity to prove their mettle."[64]

—Buffalo Bill

Several weeks later, at a college farewell dinner, it felt good to celebrate the achievements of the past seven years. From branding cattle, to my AP interview on strip clubs, to rebuilding a college, there were plenty of opportunities to walk through the fires created by the boom and the bust. On the prairie, under the majestic North Dakota sun, I hope I proved my mettle.

So, in the summer of 2016, I said good-bye. The city was hosting its second Babe Ruth World Series. And Katie Ledecky, whose family roots run deep in northwest North Dakota, was gearing up for what turned out to be a basketful of Olympic golds.

Oil was no longer king of the hill. North Dakota crude oil production fell to a 31-month low. Man camps were still fighting closure by the city. Williston and Watford City, like the bust before, had abandoned apartment buildings as a result of contractors walking away from the projects.

Workers were no longer coming to North Dakota. Protesters from across the country were beginning to flock to North Dakota to block the development of an oil pipeline. Oil protests in North Dakota had been making national headlines for several months. The US Army Corp of Engineers stopped the Dakota Access Pipeline from running through sovereign Native American lands, but one of the companies declared they would not abide by the ruling. With President Trump in office, the battle took yet another turn.

My daughter Sophia wanted to finish her last two years of high school in Williston. Joyce and I agreed. What had been a one-year transition plan had turned into a two week move from the president's house into a Foundation apartment. During the next six months, I would also fix up our Bismarck townhouse for an early spring sale, visit my father in Nashville, complete a writing assignment for the Chancellor, and write my "memoir." The official "to do" list did not include the more difficult tasks of adjusting to no longer being the president, mending fences with my wife, and saying goodbye to my terminally-ill father.

We rented a two-bedroom condo in the newly built foundation apartment. Joyce and I would take turns living in Williston with Sophia. By spending the extra time in Williston, I had the opportunity to make up for a lot of lost time with my step-daughter. My first three weeks in September did not go well. Sophia went to school early in the morning. She returned late after volleyball and pep band. We did not have much time to talk, and instead of growing closer, the alienation grew.

Joyce stayed with Sophia from mid-September to mid-October, I returned in mid-October to spend several more weeks with Sophia. Joyce told me I had to try harder. So, I woke up at the same time as Sophia. I walked her out to her car. I arranged dinners, some very late. By the end of the month, we were shopping for her winter formal dress. Maybe I didn't make up for the many years as the absent step-dad, but we did manage to reconnect.

Meanwhile in Seattle where Joyce had a large network of support, she found a position as senior corporate counsel within walking distance from home. The job was ideal as it allowed Joyce to work remotely, making her trips to Williston doable. When I wasn't in Williston to visit Sophia or Nashville to visit my father, I spent time with Julia and Emma in Seattle.

Joyce and I took the time to speak to a marriage counselor which helped immensely. Once again, we had time to reconnect. Healing is a slow process. But the love we shared before Williston was slowly returning. We even talked about renewing our vows.

I found myself in the enviable position of bonding with my two youngest daughters while writing. A friend of mine that does presidential searches contacted me twice for a job in Pennsylvania, a place she knew I had wanted to work. I declined both times. My father was dying. Joyce was getting re-established in her new job and in her element again for the first time in several years. I was getting reconnected with the girls. It was their time.

I still had one remaining commitment to the university system. Unsure of how to write the chancellor's higher education challenges and opportunities for northwest North Dakota, I began to review my personal emails, starting with my first day as president in 2009 until my resignation in 2016. I needed a method for my writing. I decided to write a memoir. On the day of the 2016, November State Board meeting, I had completed my first draft. I was excited.

In December of 2016, I presented to the chancellor my paper on the challenges and opportunities facing northwest North Dakota. His only comment was to ask whether I had shared my report with others. I responded that I had not. Given that I never again heard from Chancellor Hagerott, I can only assume that my paper was neither used nor shared. At the very least, I had fulfilled my end of our contract.

Yet... I am filled with hope. My experience of Williston was truly an epic adventure. When I remember people like Richard Stenberg, Faye Douglas, Kim Weisman, Terry Olson, Michelle Remus, Lance Olson, and so many others, I know that Williston State College, even by itself, will continue to work miracles in the turbulent and sometimes hostile oil patch. What other college could turn an oil play into a once in a lifetime scholarship for students?

There is no doubt in my mind. The resilience of the Northern Great Plains is something for the history books. I have no doubt North Dakotans will not only survive but thrive. Like metal tested in fire, they may be a little worse for the wear, but their character is truly the hardest and sharpest of blades. I have no doubt, boom or not, the community of Williston will be ready for whatever comes next. Sure, there are issues with an overburdened State Board. But my respect and admiration for the people of North Dakota has no limits. What an honor to have both served and survived.

On April 15, 2017, the man I admired most in the world, my father, passed away. For two of my dad's last four months, I had the privilege of being at his side. While my father rested, I would sit next to him writing my memoir. It did not escape me that my dad's passing came at almost the same time I finished my book, closing two significant chapters in my life.

One month later, Williston celebrated its 90th anniversary of Band Day, an annual marching band festival. I marched in the parade by walking alongside the Sons of Norway float. The float, a Viking ship, was an eye pleaser to the many Norwegians in the crowd. My job was to throw candy to the hordes of children lining the parade route which I enjoyed immensely. I wore a Norway flag t-shirt and a horned Viking helmet with mock braids. I don't believe it mattered to anyone that there is no evidence of Vikings wearing horned helmets into battle.

In rural communities across America, experiences like Band Day are quietly disappearing. But in Williston, North Dakota, where a community still relies on its collective strength, Band Day is a reminder that away from the city lights, the most important resource, even in this town that has become a city, is its community.

I will miss both my father and the community of Williston tremendously. Both have left indelible marks in my life. But strengthened by so many examples of resilience, I am prepared for my next chapter – reconnecting with Joyce and our daughters, and building upon whatever life throws at me next.

ENDNOTES

Chapter 1

[1] Walt Whitman, Complete Poetry and Collected Prose (1982 ed., p. 864, Viking Press, New York, NY).

[2] https://www.brainyquote.com/quotes/quotes/w/warrenchri 298530.html?src=t_north_dakota

[3] http://www.brainyquote.com/quotes/keywords/ north_dakota.html

[4] http://proverbicals.com/norwegian/

[5] https://en.wikipedia.org/wiki/Norwegian_Dakotan

[6] http://zipatlas.com/us/nd/williston/zip-code-comparison/percentage-norwegian-population.htm

[7] http://da1.redshift.com/~bonajo/sven.htm

[8] http://www.ndstudies.org/media/homesteading_boosterism_and_immigrants

[9] As Joyce pointed out to me, where would you take the car? There was really nowhere to take it as there was nothing for hours in any direction.

Chapter 2

[10] http://www.brainyquote.com/quotes/keywords/north_ dakota.html

[11] https://en.wikipedia.org/wiki/North_Dakota_Fighting_ Sioux_controversy

[12] http://money.cnn.com/2011/10/25/pf/America_boomtown_ strippers/

[13] http://www.motherjones.com/environment/2014/10/inside-north-dakotas-crazy-oil-boom

[14] http://www.twincities.com/2011/12/26/nudie-bars-welcome-oil-workers-to-n-d-boom-town/

[15] http://www.forbes.com/2009/06/30/north-dakota-hoeven-business-energy-economy.html

[16] http://www.governing.com/topics/energy-env/north-dakotas-oil-boom-blessing-curse.html

Chapter 3

[17] 2010, June to 2010, December

[18] http://www.ogfj.com/articles/print/volume-10/issue-4/features/what-the-frac-is-a-man-camp-.html

[19] http://www.newyorker.com/magazine/2011/04/25/kuwait-on-the-prairie

Chapter 4

[20] http://www.forbes.com/sites/christopherhelman/2011/06/27/tycoon-says-north-dakota-oil-field-will-yield-24-billion-barrels-among-worlds-biggest/#3dca5dcd7e23

[21] 2011, May to 2011, July

[22] http://www.sittingbull.org

[23] http://www.chronicle.com/article/dickinson-state-u-president/128557#list-top

[24] *Burning Glass Analysis*, System Wide Master Plan.

Chapter 5

[25] By Daniel Woods, *Williston Herald* Published/Last Modified on Monday, November 21, 2011 10:56 AM CST.

[26] http://money.cnn.com/2011/11/01/pf/America_boomtown_education/

[27] *North Dakota Quarterly Census of Employment and Wages program (QCEW), 2010 Annual Averages*

[28] http://adage.com/article/news/williston-north-dakota-town-recession-forgot/230719/

[29] http://bismarcktribune.com/news/state-and-regional/developing-minot-housing-is-a-daunting-task/article_096a1182-f2c4-11e0-9fa3-001cc4c03286.html

[30] http://www.grandforksherald.com/content/williston-state-gets-2-million.

[31] http://www.grandforksherald.com/content/williston-state-gets-2-million.

Chapter 6

[32] 2011, December to 2012, March

[33] http://www.inforum.com/content/faces-boom-nadolny-leads-williston-state-college.

[34] http://www.willistonherald.com/news/williston-schools-may-get-fema-trailers/article_cc82f4fc-72a5-11e1-92e5-001871e3ce6c.html

[35] *Monteau, Harold, North Dakota Oil Boom Bringing Jobs, Wealth—and a Looming Humanitarian Crisis, Indian County, March 15, 2012.*

[36] 1720 8th Ave E #17, Williston, Sexual assault, Garfield District Court, Colo. - Mar. 7, 2003, Angel R. nd, Risk: Low

[37] https://www.theguardian.com/cities/2014/jul/28/-sp-welcome-williston-north-dakota-america-new-gold-rush-city

[38] http://www.ibtimes.com/hard-times-boomtown-usa-rise-fall-oil-williston-north-dakota-2224834

[39] Source: Bureau of Labor Statistics Website, January 18, 2012.

Chapter 7

[40] May 2, 2013 to June 30, 2013

[41] *Business Insider, http://www.businessinsider.com/youve-never-seen-anything-like-the-williston-oil-boom-2012-3##ixzz1pOiMRXAj). March 7, 2012.*

[42] http://www.wsj.com/articles/SB10001424052702304830704577495022206535072

Chapter 8

[43] http://www.npr.org/2012/12/18/167467703/the-downsides-of-living-in-an-oil-boom-town

44 http://www.npr.org/sections/money/2013/01/10/168972151/the-north-dakota-town-where-a-one-bedroom-apartment-rents-for-2-100-a-month

45 http://www.governing.com/topics/energy-env/north-dakotas-oil-boom-blessing-curse.html

46 https://www.bloomberg.com/news/articles/2013-02-21/oil-boom-forces-employers-to-be-landlords-in-north-dakota

Chapter 9

47 http://www.thefiscaltimes.com/Articles/2013/06/06/11-Shocking-Facts-about-the-North-Dakota-Oil-Boom

48 http://www.grandforksherald.com/content/shirvani-due-more-800000-plus-health-benefits-chancellor-contract-buyout

49 http://rapidcityjournal.com/news/psst-hey-pal-want-a-job-in-north-dakota/article_4c01ae91-ecd4-5db1-a335-938eb8ada403.html

50 http://grist.org/business-technology/money-death-and-danger-in-north-dakotas-fracking-capital/#optout

51 http://www.grandforksherald.com/content/raymond-nadolny-baby-boom-marks-latest-boom-northwest-nd

Chapter 10

52 2014, July to 2014, September

53 http://www.salon.com/2014/10/09/the_overnighters_the_haunting_true_story_of_a_21st_century_boomtown/

[54] http://www.foxbusiness.com/markets/2014/10/24/high-school-grads-to-get-free-rides-at-two-year-college-in-north-dakota-oil.html

[55] http://www.crookstontimes.com/article/20141126/NEWS/141129731

Chapter 11

[56] http://www.usatoday.com/story/news/politics/2015/02/13/supreme-court-ginsburg-state-of-the-union/23360117/

Chapter 12

[57] http://money.cnn.com/2015/01/22/news/economy/oil-boomtown-layoffs/

[58] http://www.bloomberg.com/news/articles/2015-02-02/north-dakota-faces-boom-town-dilemma-as-oil-tumbles-muni-credit

[59] http://inewsnetwork.org/2015/04/03/oil-prices-are-low-but-housing-rentals-in-the-bakken-are-still-sky-high/

Chapter 13

[60] http://www.washingtontimes.com/news/2015/sep/3/higher-education-board-looks-at-rolling-back-willi/

[61] http://money.cnn.com/2016/02/02/news/economy/oil-bust-north-dakota-budget/

[62] https://chroniclevitae.com/jobs/0000311577-01

Chapter 14

[63] http://www.willistonherald.com/news/nadolny-to-resign-next-year/article_217b860a-1c56-11e6-82d1-6725496f3249.html

[64] https://www.brainyquote.com/quotes/quotes/b/buffalobil327181.html?src=t_plains

Proof

Made in the USA
Columbia, SC
25 June 2017